Box2D for Flash Games

Create amazing and realistic physics-based Flash games using Box2D

Emanuele Feronato

BIRMINGHAM - MUMBAI

Box2D for Flash Games

Copyright © 2012 Packt Publishing

All rights reserved. No part of this book may be reproduced, stored in a retrieval system, or transmitted in any form or by any means, without the prior written permission of the publisher, except in the case of brief quotations embedded in critical articles or reviews.

Every effort has been made in the preparation of this book to ensure the accuracy of the information presented. However, the information contained in this book is sold without warranty, either express or implied. Neither the author, nor Packt Publishing, and its dealers and distributors will be held liable for any damages caused or alleged to be caused directly or indirectly by this book.

Packt Publishing has endeavored to provide trademark information about all of the companies and products mentioned in this book by the appropriate use of capitals. However, Packt Publishing cannot guarantee the accuracy of this information.

First published: November 2012

Production Reference: 1161112

Published by Packt Publishing Ltd.
Livery Place
35 Livery Street
Birmingham B3 2PB, UK.

ISBN 978-1-84951-962-5

www.packtpub.com

Cover Image by Artie Ng (artherng@yahoo.com.au)

Credits

Author
Emanuele Feronato

Reviewers
Joseph Hocking
Ali Raza

Acquisition Editor
Mary Jasmine Nadar

Commissioning Editors
Priyanka Shah
Shreerang Deshpande

Technical Editor
Manmeet Singh Vasir

Copy Editor
Laxmi Subramanian

Project Coordinator
Shraddha Bagadia

Proofreaders
Maria Gould
Cecere Mario

Indexer
Hemangini Bari

Graphics
Aditi Gajjar

Production Coordinator
Prachali Bhiwandkar

Cover Work
Prachali Bhiwandkar

About the Author

Emanuele Feronato has been studying programming languages since the early 1980s, with a particular interest in game development. He taught online programming for the European Social Fund (ESF) and founded a web development company in Italy.

As a Game Developer, he has developed Flash games sponsored by the biggest game portals and his games have been played more than 70 million times, and he is now porting most of them on mobile platforms.

As a writer, he has worked as a Technical Reviewer for Packt Publishing and published the book *Flash Game Development by Example, Packt Publishing*.

His blog, www.emanueleferonato.com, is one of the most visited blogs about indie programming.

> First of all I would like to give a big thank you to Erin Catto, the guy who developed Box2D, and to Boris the Brave for porting it to AS3.
>
> A thank you also goes to Shraddha Bagadia and the entire Packt Publishing team for believing in this project, as well as to the reviewers for dealing with my drafts and improving the book.
>
> The biggest thank you obviously goes to my blog readers and to my Facebook fans for appreciating my work, giving me the will to write more and more.
>
> I also want to thank my wife Kirenia for being patient while I was writing rather than helping her to paint the house. Awesome job Kirenia!

About the Reviewers

Joseph Hocking is an interactive media developer living in Chicago. He has spent many years developing Flash games for various companies and freelance clients, and currently works for Synapse Games developing games such as Tyrant and Skyshard Heroes. His development skills include programming web-based games in AS3/Flash, using JavaScript in web pages, writing Python for both client and server applications, and building iPhone games using Lua/Corona SDK.

In addition, Joe also teaches at schools such as the Game Development program at Columbia College. Besides graphics programming, he has a great deal of training and experience in digital arts, including 3D animation. A portfolio of his work can be viewed at www.newarteest.com.

Ali Raza has a master's degree in Computer Science, and more than 8 years of experience as a Designer and Developer. He is also an Adobe Certified Instructor (ACI) and a Microsoft Certified Trainer (MCT).

He is currently working with a UK-based social networking startup as a Senior Developer (Flash Platform), and as a Consultant with a US-based firm ProContent, LLC (team behind Advanced Flash Components). In the past, he has worked with different national and international advertising, telecommunication, and IT firms.

In his free time, Ali enjoys designing and developing cross-platform desktop and mobile applications using Adobe technologies.

Ali has technically reviewed books on Adobe Flash, gaming, and HTML5. He has also published exam aids on Adobe Flex 3 and 4. He was also appointed as a Contributing Editor for Flash & Flex Developer's Magazine in 2011. He can be reached at manofspirit@gmail.com.

> I would like to express my gratitude to Packt Publishing and the author for bringing about such a wonderful title.
>
> I would also like to thank Priyanka Shah and Shraddha Bagadia for giving me the opportunity to review this amazing book on Box2D.

www.PacktPub.com

Support files, eBooks, discount offers and more

You might want to visit www.PacktPub.com for support files and downloads related to your book.

Did you know that Packt offers eBook versions of every book published, with PDF and ePub files available? You can upgrade to the eBook version at www.PacktPub.com and as a print book customer, you are entitled to a discount on the eBook copy. Get in touch with us at service@packtpub.com for more details.

At www.PacktPub.com, you can also read a collection of free technical articles, sign up for a range of free newsletters and receive exclusive discounts and offers on Packt books and eBooks.

http://PacktLib.PacktPub.com

Do you need instant solutions to your IT questions? PacktLib is Packt's online digital book library. Here, you can access, read and search across Packt's entire library of books.

Why Subscribe?

- Fully searchable across every book published by Packt
- Copy and paste, print and bookmark content
- On demand and accessible via web browser

Free Access for Packt account holders

If you have an account with Packt at www.PacktPub.com, you can use this to access PacktLib today and view nine entirely free books. Simply use your login credentials for immediate access.

I want to dedicate this book to my little daughter Kimora. I am sure she will love to read this book although at the moment she prefers Disney's picture books.

I love you "atuncita".

Table of Contents

Preface	**1**
Chapter 1: Hello Box2D World	**7**
Downloading and installing Box2D for Flash	8
Hello Box2D World	8
Defining the Box2D World	9
Running the simulation	11
Summary	14
Chapter 2: Adding Bodies to the World	**15**
Your first simulation – a ball falling on the floor	15
Creating a circular shape	17
Creating a fixture	18
Using debug draw to test your simulation	19
Creating a box shape	22
Different body types – static, dynamic, and kinematic	24
Density, friction, and restitution	26
Creating a Totem Destroyer level	28
Creating compound bodies	32
Creating an oriented box shape	34
Creating any kind of convex polygons	36
Summary	40
Chapter 3: Interacting with Bodies	**41**
Selecting and destroying bodies with a mouse click	42
Assigning custom attributes to bodies	45
Looping through bodies and getting their properties	47
Summary	52

Table of Contents

Chapter 4: Applying Forces to Bodies — 53
- Falling apples, revamped — 53
- Force, impulse, and linear velocity — 56
- Applying an impulse to get a linear velocity — 60
- Applying a force to get a linear velocity — 61
- Forces in a real game — 64
- Physics games aren't just a matter of physics — 67
- Placing the physics bird — 70
- Shooting the physics bird — 71
- Summary — 73

Chapter 5: Handling Collisions — 75
- Checking for collisions — 76
- Box2D built-in collision listener — 77
- Trace the beginning and the end of a collision — 78
- Detect when you are about to solve a collision and when you have solved it — 79
- Detecting when the idol falls on the floor in Totem Destroyer — 81
- Destroying bricks and killing pigs in Angry Birds — 85
- Summary — 91

Chapter 6: Joints and Motors — 93
- Picking and dragging bodies – mouse joints — 93
- Keeping bodies at a given distance – distance joints — 100
- Making bodies rotate around a point – revolute joints — 102
- When Angry Birds meets Crush the Castle — 105
- Controlling joints with motors — 110
- Controlling motors with keyboard — 113
- Don't let some bodies collide – filtering collisions — 117
- Putting it all together — 122
- Summary — 127

Chapter 7: Skinning the Game — 129
- Replacing debug draw with your own graphic assets — 129
- Summary — 136

Chapter 8: Bullets and Sensors — 137
- Experiencing tunneling — 138
- Preventing tunneling – setting bodies as bullets — 140
- Allow bodies to overlap while detecting contacts with sensors — 142
- Summary — 145

Index — 147

Preface

If you look at the most successful Flash games, most of them use physics to add realism and features, which would not have been possible otherwise. This book will guide you through the creation of physics games using Box2D, a free open source physics engine, which is the most used one among game developers. Throughout the book, you will learn how to use Box2D while you create real games.

What this book covers

Chapter 1, *Hello Box2D World*, introduces what is Box2D, what you can do with it, how to include it in your Flash projects, and your first Box2D world.

Chapter 2, *Adding Bodies to the World*, explains how to add primitive and complex bodies to the world, and see them displayed on the stage. It also introduces units of measurement.

Chapter 3, *Interacting with Bodies*, looks at showing how to interact with bodies, selecting them with the mouse, and knowing their position in the world.

Chapter 4, *Applying Forces to Bodies*, explains how forces and impulses make bodies move in the Box2D world, and how to apply them to animate the world.

Chapter 5, *Handling Collisions*, answers questions such as: did two bodies collide, was it a hard collision, and where did they collide. We will also discover how to handle collisions among bodies.

Chapter 6, *Joints and Motors*, explains how to create complex structures using joints, and give them a life applying motors.

Preface

Chapter 7, Skinning the Game, explains how to render Box2D world using your own graphic assets.

Chapter 8, Bullets and Sensors, discusses the need for bodies with special attributes. It also explains how to use bullets and sensors for a more accurate simulation and for silent collisions.

What you need for this book

Flash CS5 or above is needed. You can download a fully functional free trial of Adobe Flash Professional CS6 from www.adobe.com/go/tryflash/.

Who this book is for

Do you already know AS3 basics and want to add to your games a great twist, thanks to physics? Then this book is for you, even if you don't know physics.

Conventions

In this book, you will find a number of styles of text that distinguish between different kinds of information. Here are some examples of these styles, and an explanation of their meaning.

Code words in text are shown as follows: "Nothing new, we just added an ENTER_FRAME event, but we needed it in order to run the simulation inside the updateWorld function."

A block of code is set as follows:

```
package {
  import flash.display.Sprite
  import Box2D.Dynamics.*;
  import Box2D.Collision.*;
  import Box2D.Collision.Shapes.*;
  import Box2D.Common.Math.*;
  public class Main extends Sprite {
    public function Main() {
      trace("my awesome game starts here");
    }
  }
}
```

When we wish to draw your attention to a particular part of a code block, the relevant lines or items are set in bold:

```
package {
  import flash.display.Sprite;
  import flash.events.Event;
  import Box2D.Dynamics.*;
  import Box2D.Collision.*;
  import Box2D.Collision.Shapes.*;
  import Box2D.Common.Math.*;
  public class Main extends Sprite {
    public function Main() {
      var gravity:b2Vec2=new b2Vec2(0,9.81);
      var sleep:Boolean=true;
      var world:b2World = new b2World(gravity,sleep);
      addEventListener(Event.ENTER_FRAME,updateWorld);
    }
    private function updateWorld(e:Event):void {
      trace("my awesome simulation runs here");
    }
  }
}
```

New terms and **important words** are shown in bold. Words that you see on the screen, in menus or dialog boxes for example, appear in the text like this: "Please notice the names under **AS Linkage** as I will be using them in the code."

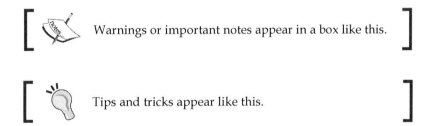

[Warnings or important notes appear in a box like this.]

[Tips and tricks appear like this.]

Reader feedback

Feedback from our readers is always welcome. Let us know what you think about this book—what you liked or may have disliked. Reader feedback is important for us to develop titles that you really get the most out of.

To send us general feedback, simply send an e-mail to feedback@packtpub.com, and mention the book title through the subject of your message.

If there is a topic that you have expertise in and you are interested in either writing or contributing to a book, see our author guide on www.packtpub.com/authors.

Customer support

Now that you are the proud owner of a Packt book, we have a number of things to help you to get the most from your purchase.

Downloading the example code

You can download the example code files for all Packt books you have purchased from your account at http://www.packtpub.com. If you purchased this book elsewhere, you can visit http://www.packtpub.com/support and register to have the files e-mailed directly to you.

Errata

Although we have taken every care to ensure the accuracy of our content, mistakes do happen. If you find a mistake in one of our books—maybe a mistake in the text or the code—we would be grateful if you would report this to us. By doing so, you can save other readers from frustration and help us improve subsequent versions of this book. If you find any errata, please report them by visiting http://www.packtpub.com/support, selecting your book, clicking on the **errata submission form** link, and entering the details of your errata. Once your errata are verified, your submission will be accepted and the errata will be uploaded to our website, or added to any list of existing errata, under the Errata section of that title.

Piracy

Piracy of copyright material on the Internet is an ongoing problem across all media. At Packt, we take the protection of our copyright and licenses very seriously. If you come across any illegal copies of our works, in any form, on the Internet, please provide us with the location address or website name immediately so that we can pursue a remedy.

Please contact us at `copyright@packtpub.com` with a link to the suspected pirated material.

We appreciate your help in protecting our authors, and our ability to bring you valuable content.

Questions

You can contact us at `questions@packtpub.com` if you are having a problem with any aspect of the book, and we will do our best to address it.

Hello Box2D World

If you want to create 2D physics-driven games and applications, Box2D is the best choice available. **Box2D** is a 2D rigid body simulation library used in some of the most successful games, such as Angry Birds and Tiny Wings on iPhone or Totem Destroyer and Red Remover on Flash. Google them, and you'll see a lot of enthusiastic reviews.

Before we dive into the Box2D World, let me explain what is a **rigid body**. It's a piece of matter that is so strong that it can't be bent in any way. There is no way to modify its shape, no matter how hard you hit it or throw it. In the real world, you can think about something as hard as a diamond, or even more. Matter coming from outer space that can't be deformed.

Box2D only manages rigid bodies, which will be called just "bodies" from now on, but don't worry, you will also be able to simulate stuff which normally is not rigid, such as bouncing balls.

Let's see what you are about to learn in this chapter:

- Downloading and installing Box2D for Flash
- Including required classes in your Flash projects
- Creating your first Box2D World
- Understanding gravity and sleeping bodies
- Running your first empty simulation, handling time steps, and constraints

By the end of the chapter, you will be able to create an empty, yet running world where you can build your awesome physics games.

Downloading and installing Box2D for Flash

You can download the latest version of Box2D for Flash either from the official site (http://www.box2dflash.org/download) or from the SourceForge project page (http://sourceforge.net/projects/box2dflash/).

Once you have downloaded the zipped package, extract the Box2D folder (you can find it inside the Source folder) into the same folder you are using for your project. The following is how your awesome game folder should look before you start coding:

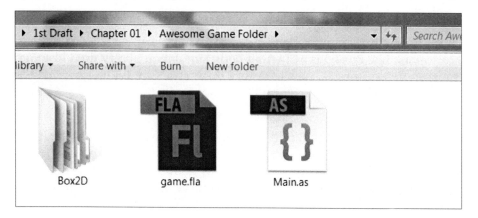

You can see the Box2D folder, the FLA file that I am assuming has a document class called Main and therefore Main.as, which is the class we will work on.

I would suggest you work on a 640 x 480 Flash movie at 30 **frames per second (fps)**. The document class should be called Main and the examples will look better if you use a dark stage background color, such as #333333. At least these are the settings I am using throughout the book. Obviously you can change them as you want, but in that case your final movies may look a bit different than the examples shown in the book.

Now let's import Box2D classes.

Hello Box2D World

Box2D is free and open source, so you won't need to install components or deal with SWC files. All you need to do to include it in your projects is to include the required classes.

Open `Main.as` and write the following code snippet:

```
package {
  import flash.display.Sprite
  import Box2D.Dynamics.*;
  import Box2D.Collision.*;
  import Box2D.Collision.Shapes.*;
  import Box2D.Common.Math.*;
  public class Main extends Sprite {
    public function Main() {
      trace("my awesome game starts here");
    }
  }
}
```

Test the movie and you should see **my awesome game starts here** in your **Output** window. This means you have successfully imported the required classes.

There isn't that much to say about the code we just wrote, as we are just importing the classes needed to make our Box2D project work.

When I gave the *Hello Box2D World* title, I did not mean to create just another "Hello World" section, but I wanted to introduce the environment where all Box2D simulation and events take place: the **world**.

The world is the stage where the simulation happens. Everything you want to be ruled by the Box2D physics must be inside the world. Luckily, the Box2D World is always big enough to contain everything you need, so you don't have to worry about world boundaries. Just remember everything on a computer has limits in one way or another. So, the bigger the world, the heavier will be the work for your computer to manage it.

Defining the Box2D World

Like all worlds, the Box2D World has a **gravity**, so the first thing you need to do is define world gravity.

1. In your `Main` function, add the following line:

   ```
   var gravity:b2Vec2=new b2Vec2(0,9.81);
   ```

   This introduces our first Box2D data type: `b2Vec2`.

b2Vec2 is a 2D column vector that is a data type, which will store x and y components of a vector. As you can see, the constructor has two arguments, both numbers, representing the x and y components. This way we are defining the gravity variable as a vector with x=0 (which means no horizontal gravity) and y=-9.81 (which approximates Earth gravity).

Physics says the speed of an object falling freely near the Earth's surface increases by about 9.81 meters per second squared, which might be thought of as "meters per second, per second". So assuming there isn't any air resistance, we are about to simulate a real-world environment. Explaining the whole theory of a falling body is beyond the scope of this book, but you can get more information by searching for "equations for a falling body" on Google or Wikipedia.

2. You can set your game on the move with the following line:

   ```
   var gravity:b2Vec2=new b2Vec2(0,1.63);
   ```

   You can also simulate a no gravity environment with the arguments set at (0,0):

   ```
   var gravity:b2Vec2=new b2Vec2(0,0);
   ```

   Working with no gravity is also useful if you want to work in a top-down environment.

3. We also need to tell if bodies inside the world are allowed to **sleep** when they come to rest, that is when they aren't affected by forces. A sleeping body does not require simulation, it just rests in its position as its presence does not affect anything in the world, allowing Box2D to ignore it, and thus speeding up the processing time and letting us achieve a better performance. So I always recommend to put bodies to sleep when possible.

   Sleeping bodies won't sleep forever and they'll wake up as soon as a collision occurs or a force is applied directly on them.

4. Add the following line, which is just a simple Boolean variable definition:

   ```
   var sleep:Boolean=true;
   ```

5. And finally, we are ready to create our first world:

   ```
   var world:b2World = new b2World(gravity,sleep);
   ```

6. Now we have a container to manage all the bodies and perform our dynamic simulation.

7. Time to make a small recap. At the moment, your code should look like the following:

```
package {
  import flash.display.Sprite;
  import Box2D.Dynamics.*;
  import Box2D.Collision.*;
  import Box2D.Collision.Shapes.*;
  import Box2D.Common.Math.*;
  public class Main extends Sprite {
    public function Main() {
      var gravity:b2Vec2=new b2Vec2(0,9.81);
      var sleep:Boolean=true;
      var world:b2World = new b2World(gravity,sleep);
    }
  }
}
```

Now you learned how to create and configure a Box2D World. Let's see how can you simulate physics in it.

Running the simulation

You need to run the simulation at every frame, so first of all you need a listener to be triggered at every frame.

1. Let's make some simple changes to our class:

```
package {
  import flash.display.Sprite;
  import flash.events.Event;
  import Box2D.Dynamics.*;
  import Box2D.Collision.*;
  import Box2D.Collision.Shapes.*;
  import Box2D.Common.Math.*;
  public class Main extends Sprite {
    public function Main() {
      var gravity:b2Vec2=new b2Vec2(0,9.81);
      var sleep:Boolean=true;
      var world:b2World = new b2World(gravity,sleep);
      addEventListener(Event.ENTER_FRAME,updateWorld);
    }
    private function updateWorld(e:Event):void {
      trace("my awesome simulation runs here");
    }
  }
}
```

Nothing new, we just added an ENTER_FRAME event, but we needed it in order to run the simulation inside the updateWorld function. If you have doubts regarding event handling with AS3, refer to the official Adobe docs or get *Flash Game Development by Example*, Packt Publishing, which will guide you to a step-by-step creation of pure AS3 games.

Box2D simulation works by simulating the world at discrete steps of time. This means the world gets updated at every time step. It's up to us to decide which time step we are going to use for our simulation. Normally, physics in games have a time step of 1/60 seconds. Anyway, as I am running the Flash movie at 30 fps, I am going to set a time step of 1/30 seconds.

2. The first line into the updateWorld function will be:

   ```
   var timeStep:Number=1/30
   ```

   Just defining a time step, is not enough. At every step, every physic entity is updated according to the forces acting on it (unless it's sleeping). The algorithm which handles this task is called **constraint solver**. It basically loops through each constraint and solves it, one at a time. If you want to learn more about constraints, search for "constraint algorithm" on Google or Wikipedia.

   Where's the catch? While a single constraint is solved perfectly, it can mess with other constraints that have already been solved.

   Think about two balls moving: in the real world, each ball position is updated at the same time. In a computer simulation, we need to loop through the balls and update their position one at a time. Think about a for loop that updates a ball at every iteration. Everything works as long as the balls do not interact with each other, but what happens if the second ball hits the first, whose position has already been updated? They would overlap, which is not possible in a rigid body simulation.

   To solve this problem with a reasonable approximation, we need to loop over all the constraints more than once. Now the question is: how many times?

   There are two constraint solvers: **velocity constraint solver** and **position constraint solver**. The velocity solver is used to move physic entities in the world according to their impulses. The position solver adjusts physic entities' positions to avoid overlap.

   So it's obvious that the more iterations there are, the more accurate the simulation, and the lower will be the performance. I managed to handle more than 100 physic entities using 10 velocity and position iterations, although the author of Box2D recommends 8 for velocity and 3 for position.

3. It's up to you to play with these values. Meanwhile, I'll be using 10 iterations for both constraint solvers.

   So here we go with two new variables:

   ```
   var velIterations:int=10;
   var posIterations:int=10;
   ```

4. Finally we are ready to call the Step method on the world variable to update the simulation.

   To use world inside the updateWorld function, we need to declare world as a class-level variable, shown as follows:

   ```
   package {
     import flash.display.Sprite;
     import flash.events.Event;
     import Box2D.Dynamics.*;
     import Box2D.Collision.*;
     import Box2D.Collision.Shapes.*;
     import Box2D.Common.Math.*;
     public class Main extends Sprite {
       private var world:b2World;
       public function Main() {
         var gravity:b2Vec2=new b2Vec2(0,9.81);
         var sleep:Boolean=true;
         world=new b2World(gravity,sleep);
         addEventListener(Event.ENTER_FRAME,updateWorld);
       }
       private function updateWorld(e:Event):void {
         var timeStep:Number=1/30;
         var velIterations:int=10;
         var posIterations:int=10;
         world.Step(timeStep,velIterations,posIterations);
       }
     }
   }
   ```

   Now we have our world configured and running. Unfortunately, it's a very boring world, with nothing in it. So in the next chapter, we are going to populate the world with all kinds of physic entities.

5. Just one last thing, after each step you need to clear forces, to let the simulation start again at the next step.

Hello Box2D World

6. You can do it by adding the following line right after the `Step` method:

   `world.ClearForces();` Your final code is shown as follows:

```
package {
  import flash.display.Sprite;
  import flash.events.Event;
  import Box2D.Dynamics.*;
  import Box2D.Collision.*;
  import Box2D.Collision.Shapes.*;
  import Box2D.Common.Math.*;
  public class Main extends Sprite {
    private var world:b2World;
    public function Main() {
      var gravity:b2Vec2=new b2Vec2(0,9.81);
      var sleep:Boolean=true;
      world=new b2World(gravity,sleep);
      addEventListener(Event.ENTER_FRAME,updateWorld);
    }
    private function updateWorld(e:Event):void {
      var timeStep:Number=1/30;
      var velIterations:int=10;
      var posIterations:int=10;
      world.Step(timeStep,velIterations,posIterations);
      world.ClearForces();
    }
  }
}
```

> **Downloading the example code**
>
> You can download the example code files for all Packt books you have purchased from your account at http://www.packtpub.com. If you purchased this book elsewhere, you can visit http://www.packtpub.com/support and register to have the files e-mailed directly to you.

And now you are really ready to place some action in your Box2D World.

Summary

You have just learned how to install Box2D for Flash. Include it in your projects and create a running, gravity-ruled simulation managing time steps and constraint solvers.

You have an empty world ready to be the container where your awesome game will take place. Save it and use it in every future project!

2
Adding Bodies to the World

Bodies are what make Box2D games possible. Anything you can move or interact with, is a **body**. Birds, pigs, and crates in Angry Birds are bodies, as well as the idol and the totem bricks in Totem Destroyer.

During this chapter, you will learn to create every kind of Box2D body, in addition to some other important features, including:

- Creating circular bodies
- Creating rectangular bodies
- Creating any kind of polygon
- Using debug draw to test your simulation
- Defining body types: static, dynamic, or kinematic
- Setting material attributes: density, friction, and restitution
- Units of measurement
- Creating compound objects

By the end of the chapter, you will have your first Totem Destroyer level ready to play with. This will be a long chapter, so let's drive straight to the point.

Your first simulation – a ball falling on the floor

We are starting with an easy task, the simplest of all physics simulations: a ball falling on the floor. Anyway, although it's just another falling ball, being your first simulation this will be quite an achievement.

Adding Bodies to the World

Let's see what we have in our simulation:

- A world with a gravity
- A ball that should react to world forces (such as gravity)
- A floor that shouldn't react to world forces
- Some kind of materials, as we expect the ball to bounce on the floor

You are already able to configure a world with gravity, so we are going to start with the creation of the ball.

1. It doesn't matter if we are creating a sphere or a polygon, the first step to create a body is:

   ```
   var bodyDef:b2BodyDef=new b2BodyDef();
   ```

   `b2BodyDef` is the body definition, which will hold all data needed to create our rigid body.

2. Now it's time to place the body somewhere in the world. As we are working on a 640 x 480 size, we'll place the ball in the top-center position of the stage, let's say at (320,30), shown as follows:

   ```
   bodyDef.position.Set(10.66,1);
   ```

   The `position` property obviously sets the body's position in the world, but I am sure you are wondering why I told you that I was going to place the body at (320,30) and instead placed it at (10.66,1). It's a matter of units of measurement. While Flash works with *pixels*, Box2D tries to simulate the real world and works with *meters*. There isn't a general rule for converting pixels to meters, but we can say that the following equation works well:

   meters = pixels * 30

   So, if we define a variable to help us with the conversion from meters to pixels, we can use pixels rather than meters when dealing with the Box2D World. This is more intuitive for all of us who are used to thinking in pixels when making Flash games.

3. Open the class you have created in the first chapter and change it in the following way:

   ```
   package {
     import flash.display.Sprite;
     import flash.events.Event;
     import Box2D.Dynamics.*;
     import Box2D.Collision.*;
     import Box2D.Collision.Shapes.*;
     import Box2D.Common.Math.*;
   ```

```
public class Main extends Sprite {
  private var world:b2World;
  private var worldScale:Number=30;
  public function Main() {
    world=new b2World(new b2Vec2(0,9.81),true);
    var bodyDef:b2BodyDef=new b2BodyDef();
    bodyDef.position.Set(320/worldScale,30/worldScale);
    addEventListener(Event.ENTER_FRAME,updateWorld);
  }
  private function updateWorld(e:Event):void {
    world.Step(1/30,10,10);
    world.ClearForces();

  }
 }
}
```

Also, notice how I created the world and called the Step method. It's just to save some lines of code.

Once you're done with the creation of a body definition, it's time to give it a shape.

Creating a circular shape

A **shape** is a 2D geometrical object, such as a circle or a polygon, which in this case must be *convex* (every internal angle must be less than 180 degrees). Remember, Box2D can *only* handle convex shapes.

At the moment, we are starting with the ball, so we'll create the circle:

```
var circleShape:b2CircleShape;
circleShape=new b2CircleShape(25/worldScale);
```

b2CircleShape is used to create a circular shape, and its constructor wants the radius as an argument. With the previous lines, we are creating a circle whose radius is 25 pixels, thanks to our friend — the worldScale variable. From now on, every time you want to work with pixels, you'll have to divide them by worldScale. You can also define a function called, let's say, pixelsToMeters, and call it every time you need to convert pixels to meters.

When we have a body definition and a shape, we can glue them together using a fixture.

Adding Bodies to the World

Creating a fixture

A **fixture** is used to bind the shape on a body, and to define its material setting density, friction, and restitution. Don't worry about materials at the moment, and let's focus on the fixture.

1. The first step is to create the fixture:
   ```
   var fixtureDef:b2FixtureDef = new b2FixtureDef();
   fixtureDef.shape=circleShape;
   ```
   Once we have created the fixture with the constructor, we assign the previously created shape using the `shape` property.

2. Finally we are ready to add the ball to the world:
   ```
   var theBall:b2Body=world.CreateBody(bodyDef);
   theBall.CreateFixture(fixtureDef);
   ```
   `b2Body` is the body itself: the physical, concrete body that has been created using the `bodyDef` attribute.

3. To recap, use the following steps when you want to place a body in the world:
   i. Create a body definition, which will hold body information such as its position.
   ii. Create a shape, which is how the body will look.
   iii. Create a fixture to attach the shape to the body definition.
   iv. Create the body itself in the world using the fixture.

   Once you know the importance of each step, adding bodies to your Box2D World will be easy and fun.

4. Back to our project. The following is how the class should look now:
   ```
   package {
     import flash.display.Sprite;
     import flash.events.Event;
     import Box2D.Dynamics.*;
     import Box2D.Collision.*;
     import Box2D.Collision.Shapes.*;
     import Box2D.Common.Math.*;
     public class Main extends Sprite {
       private var world:b2World;
       private var worldScale:Number=30;
       public function Main() {
   ```

```
            world=new b2World(new b2Vec2(0,9.81),true);
            var bodyDef:b2BodyDef=new b2BodyDef();
            bodyDef.position.Set(320/worldScale,30/worldScale);
            var circleShape:b2CircleShape;
            circleShape=new b2CircleShape(25/worldScale);
            var fixtureDef:b2FixtureDef = new b2FixtureDef();
            fixtureDef.shape=circleShape;
            var theBall:b2Body=world.CreateBody(bodyDef);
            theBall.CreateFixture(fixtureDef);
            addEventListener(Event.ENTER_FRAME,updateWorld);
        }
        private function updateWorld(e:Event):void {
            world.Step(1/30,10,10);
            world.ClearForces;
        }
    }
}
```

Time to save the project and test it. Ready to see your first Box2D body in action? Run the movie!

Ok, it did not display anything. Before you throw this book, let me tell you that Box2D only *simulates* the physic world, but it *does not display* anything.

This means your body is alive and kicking in your Box2D World; it's just that you can't see it.

Using debug draw to test your simulation

Luckily, Box2D comes with a feature, **debug draw**, that will help us to see what's going on.

1. Debug draw will display what happens in the Box2D World, and we can enable it by calling world's `DrawDebugData` method right after the `Step` method, in the `updateWorld` function:

    `world.DrawDebugData();`

2. Once we've told the world to display the debug draw after each iteration, we need to define the visual settings used by debug draw. Add the following lines to your `Main` class:

   ```
   package {
     import flash.display.Sprite;
     import flash.events.Event;
     import Box2D.Dynamics.*;
   ```

Adding Bodies to the World

```
import Box2D.Collision.*;
import Box2D.Collision.Shapes.*;
import Box2D.Common.Math.*;
public class Main extends Sprite {
  private var world:b2World;
  private var worldScale:Number=30;
  public function Main() {
    world =new b2World(new b2Vec2(0,9.81),true);
    var bodyDef:b2BodyDef=new b2BodyDef();
    bodyDef.position.Set(320/worldScale,30/worldScale);
    var circleShape:b2CircleShape;
    circleShape=new b2CircleShape(25/worldScale);
    var fixtureDef:b2FixtureDef = new b2FixtureDef();
    fixtureDef.shape=circleShape;
    var theBall:b2Body=world.CreateBody(bodyDef);
    theBall.CreateFixture(fixtureDef);
    var debugDraw:b2DebugDraw = new b2DebugDraw();
    var debugSprite:Sprite = new Sprite();
    addChild(debugSprite);
    debugDraw.SetSprite(debugSprite);
    debugDraw.SetDrawScale(worldScale);
    debugDraw.SetFlags(b2DebugDraw.e_shapeBit);
    debugDraw.SetFillAlpha(0.5);
    world.SetDebugDraw(debugDraw);
    addEventListener(Event.ENTER_FRAME,updateWorld);
  }
  private function updateWorld(e:Event):void {
    world.Step(1/30,10,10);
    world.ClearForces();
    world.DrawDebugData();
  }
 }
}
```

3. That's a lot of stuff, so let's explain what has happened. You already know what `DrawDebugData` stands for, so we are going to see the meaning of the other lines:

   ```
   var debugDraw:b2DebugDraw = new b2DebugDraw();
   ```

   `b2DebugDraw` is the class that provides debug drawing of physics entities in your game.

   ```
   var debugSprite:Sprite = new Sprite();
   ```

`debugSprite` is just a sprite; the canvas used to display debug draw data.

`addChild(debugSprite);`

Debug draw sprite is added to Display List, ready to be shown on stage.

`debugDraw.SetSprite(debugSprite);`

The `SetSprite` method tells which sprite will be used to display debug draw.

`debugDraw.SetDrawScale(worldScale);`

As we are converting meters to pixels, we need to tell debug draw the draw scale we are using.

`debugDraw.SetFlags(b2DebugDraw.e_shapeBit);`

The `SetFlags` method allows us to decide which kind of physic entities we are going to represent with debug draw. At this moment we only need to draw the shapes.

`debugDraw.SetFillAlpha(0.5);`

The `SetFillAlpha` method is used just for an aesthetic purpose. This way shape's outline will be fully opaque while their fill color will be semitransparent. This makes the debug draw output more understandable.

`world.SetDebugDraw(debugDraw);`

Finally, we assign the debug draw we just created to the world.

4. Now it's time to test your movie, and you should finally see the ball:

Adding Bodies to the World

That's it! You managed to see the bodies you have placed into Box2D World.

At the moment the ball does not seem to fall down according to gravity, but don't worry about it now, we'll fix it later.

Now, let's create something that can be used as a ground, such as a large rectangle to be placed at the bottom-side of the stage. Everything will be simpler from now on, as new bodies will be automatically displayed as soon as they are added to the world.

Creating a box shape

Let's perform the following steps:

1. First, body and fixture definitions can be reassigned to define our new body. This way, we don't need to declare another `bodyDef` variable, but we just need to reuse the one we used for the creation of the sphere by changing its position:

   ```
   bodyDef.position.Set(320/worldScale,470/worldScale);
   ```

   Now the body definition is located in the horizontal center, and close to the bottom of the screen.

2. To create a polygon shape, we will use the `b2PolygonShape` class:

   ```
   var polygonShape:b2PolygonShape=new b2PolygonShape();
   ```

   This way we create a polygon shape in the same way we created the circle shape earlier.

3. Polygon shapes must follow some restrictions, but at the moment because we only need an axis-aligned box, the `SetAsBox` method is all we need.

   ```
   polygonShape.SetAsBox(320/worldScale,10/worldScale);
   ```

   The method requires two arguments: the half-width and the half-height of the box. In the end, our new polygon shape will have its center at pixels (320, 470), and it will have a width of 640 pixels and a height of 20 pixels—just what we need to create a floor.

4. Now we change the `shape` attribute of the fixture definition, attaching the new polygon shape:

   ```
   fixtureDef.shape=polygonShape;
   ```

5. Finally, we can create the world body and embed the fixture in it, just like we did with the sphere.

   ```
   var theFloor:b2Body=world.CreateBody(bodyDef);
   theFloor.CreateFixture(fixtureDef);
   ```

Chapter 2

6. The following is how your `Main` function should look now:

```
public function Main() {
  world=new b2World(new b2Vec2(0,9.81),true);
  var bodyDef:b2BodyDef=new b2BodyDef();
  bodyDef.position.Set(320/worldScale,30/worldScale);
  var circleShape:b2CircleShape;
  circleShape=new b2CircleShape(25/worldScale);
  var fixtureDef:b2FixtureDef=new b2FixtureDef();
  fixtureDef.shape=circleShape;
  var theBall:b2Body=world.CreateBody(bodyDef);
  theBall.CreateFixture(fixtureDef);
  bodyDef.position.Set(320/worldScale,470/worldScale);
  var polygonShape:b2PolygonShape=new b2PolygonShape();
  polygonShape.SetAsBox(320/worldScale,10/worldScale);
  fixtureDef.shape=polygonShape;
  var theFloor:b2Body=world.CreateBody(bodyDef);
  theFloor.CreateFixture(fixtureDef);
  var debugDraw:b2DebugDraw=new b2DebugDraw();
  var debugSprite:Sprite=new Sprite();
  addChild(debugSprite);
  debugDraw.SetSprite(debugSprite);
  debugDraw.SetDrawScale(worldScale);
  debugDraw.SetFlags(b2DebugDraw.e_shapeBit);
  debugDraw.SetFillAlpha(0.5);
  world.SetDebugDraw(debugDraw);
  addEventListener(Event.ENTER_FRAME,updateWorld);
}
```

7. Test the movie and you'll see the floor:

Adding Bodies to the World

Can you see how easy it is? We took almost a chapter and an half to place our first body, and just a few more lines to add another body.

Now it's time to worry about gravity, as the ball should fall down.

Different body types – static, dynamic, and kinematic

There are three types of Box2D bodies: static, dynamic, and kinematic.

A **static** body does not react to any force, impulse, or collision and does not move. A static body can only be moved manually by the user. By default, every Box2D body is a static body, and that's why the ball does not move. A static body also does not collide with other static or kinematic bodies.

A **dynamic** body reacts to forces, impulses, collisions, and any other world event. Dynamic bodies can also be moved manually, although I'd suggest to let them be moved by world forces, and collide with all body types.

A **kinematic** body is something hybrid between a static and a dynamic body. Kinematic bodies do not react to forces, but can be moved both manually and by setting their velocity. Kinematic bodies do not collide with other static or kinematic bodies.

Back to our simulation now. Which type of body would you assign to the ball and the floor?

The floor must be a static body, as it does not have to move, while the ball will be a dynamic body to be moved by world forces.

To tell Box2D the type of each body, you just have to set the `type` property of the body definition, which can be `b2Body.b2_staticBody`, `b2Body.b2_dynamicBody`, or `b2Body.b2_kinematicBody` respectively for static, dynamic, or kinematic bodies.

Your new `Main` function is shown as follows:

```
public function Main() {
   world=new b2World(new b2Vec2(0,9.81),true);
   var bodyDef:b2BodyDef=new b2BodyDef();
   bodyDef.position.Set(320/worldScale,30/worldScale);
   bodyDef.type=b2Body.b2_dynamicBody;
   var circleShape:b2CircleShape;
   circleShape=new b2CircleShape(25/worldScale);
   var fixtureDef:b2FixtureDef=new b2FixtureDef();
```

```
        fixtureDef.shape=circleShape;
        var theBall:b2Body=world.CreateBody(bodyDef);
        theBall.CreateFixture(fixtureDef);
        bodyDef.position.Set(320/worldScale,470/worldScale);
        bodyDef.type=b2Body.b2_staticBody;
        var polygonShape:b2PolygonShape=new b2PolygonShape();
        polygonShape.SetAsBox(320/worldScale,10/worldScale);
        fixtureDef.shape=polygonShape;
        var theFloor:b2Body=world.CreateBody(bodyDef);
        theFloor.CreateFixture(fixtureDef);
        var debugDraw:b2DebugDraw=new b2DebugDraw();
        var debugSprite:Sprite=new Sprite();
        addChild(debugSprite);
        debugDraw.SetSprite(debugSprite);
        debugDraw.SetDrawScale(worldScale);
        debugDraw.SetFlags(b2DebugDraw.e_shapeBit);
        debugDraw.SetFillAlpha(0.5);
        world.SetDebugDraw(debugDraw);
        addEventListener(Event.ENTER_FRAME,updateWorld);
    }
```

Now the ball should fall down. Test the movie and see:

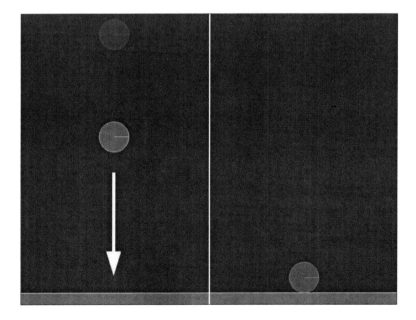

Before the congratulations for running your first simulation, let me spend to say a couple of words about different colors you will see when using the debug draw.

Adding Bodies to the World

Static bodies will be drawn in **green**. Dynamic bodies will be drawn in **red** when they're not sleeping and in **gray** where they are put to sleep. Kinematic bodies, not shown in the previous screenshot, will be drawn with **blue**.

Now it should also clear the concept of putting bodies to sleep and saving CPU work. As you can see, when the ball hits the ground, no other forces are acting on it, so it can be put to sleep until something happens.

Now, a new problem. The ball did not bounce. We need to give our bodies some more attributes if we want to run a complete simulation.

Density, friction, and restitution

As you already know how to add bodies to the world, I want to introduce you to three attributes that will affect bodies' behavior: density, friction, and restitution.

The **density** is used to set the mass of a body, measured in kilograms by square meter. Higher density means heavier bodies, and it can't be negative.

The **friction** comes into play when two bodies slide on each other, and it's defined by a coefficient, usually from 0 (no friction) to 1 (strong friction). It can't be negative.

The **restitution** determines how much a body will bounce after a collision. Like density and friction, it can't be negative and it's defined by a coefficient usually from 0 to 1. A ball falling on the ground with restitution zero won't bounce (**inelastic collision**), whereas a value of one would have made the ball bounce with the same velocity it had at the moment of the collision (**perfectly elastic collision**).

```
Density, friction, and restitution must be added to the fixture,
so change the Main function by adding the following lines:public
function Main() {
  world=new b2World(new b2Vec2(0,9.81),true);
  var bodyDef:b2BodyDef=new b2BodyDef();
  bodyDef.position.Set(320/worldScale,30/worldScale);
  bodyDef.type=b2Body.b2_dynamicBody;
  var circleShape:b2CircleShape;
  circleShape=new b2CircleShape(25/worldScale);
  var fixtureDef:b2FixtureDef=new b2FixtureDef();
  fixtureDef.shape=circleShape;
  fixtureDef.density=1;
  fixtureDef.restitution=0.6;
  fixtureDef.friction=0.1;
  var theBall:b2Body=world.CreateBody(bodyDef);
  theBall.CreateFixture(fixtureDef);
  bodyDef.position.Set(320/worldScale,470/worldScale);
```

```
        bodyDef.type=b2Body.b2_staticBody;
        var polygonShape:b2PolygonShape=new b2PolygonShape();
        polygonShape.SetAsBox(320/worldScale,10/worldScale);
        fixtureDef.shape=polygonShape;
        var theFloor:b2Body=world.CreateBody(bodyDef);
        theFloor.CreateFixture(fixtureDef);
        var debugDraw:b2DebugDraw=new b2DebugDraw();
        var debugSprite:Sprite=new Sprite();
        addChild(debugSprite);
        debugDraw.SetSprite(debugSprite);
        debugDraw.SetDrawScale(worldScale);
        debugDraw.SetFlags(b2DebugDraw.e_shapeBit);
        debugDraw.SetFillAlpha(0.5);
        world.SetDebugDraw(debugDraw);
        addEventListener(Event.ENTER_FRAME,updateWorld);
    }
```

I am assigning the attributes only once, so both bodies will have the same fixture attributes. We'll deal a lot with fixture attributes during the course of this book, so at the moment let's just make this ball bounce.

Test the movie and you should see the ball bouncing.

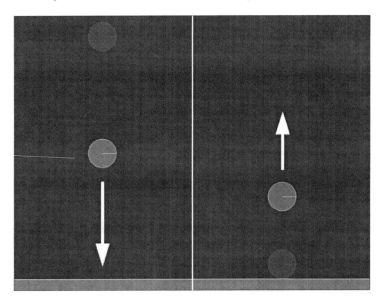

Congratulations! You just completed your first real Box2D project, and now you are able to create basic shapes and assign their attributes and properties.

It's time to create something closer to a game.

Creating a Totem Destroyer level

Now you have the skills to create your first game prototype, and we are going to start with a Totem Destroyer level.

To show you we are doing things for real, we will take a real level of the popular Flash game Totem Destroyer, and reproduce an exactly similar one. Look at the following screenshot:

Totem Destroyer: Gabriel Ochsenhofer (www.gabs.tv)

This is the first level of the original Totem Destroyer game, and if you look at it you will find bricks of a size which are multiples of 30. Can you figure out why? Yes, it's simple, because of the meters to pixels conversion.

The author probably created the game working directly with meters, but we are sticking to our guns and working with pixels.

At the moment we don't need to worry about brown and black pixels, we just want to reproduce the totem.

Before we start coding, for the sake of simplicity, I would suggest you create a couple of functions that will help us to reuse the code. Don't worry, there's nothing new, we are just organizing a bit in the script.

1. So we will have a `debugDraw` function that will handle every debug draw related code:

```
private function debugDraw():void {
    var debugDraw:b2DebugDraw=new b2DebugDraw();
    var debugSprite:Sprite=new Sprite();
```

```
    addChild(debugSprite);
    debugDraw.SetSprite(debugSprite);
    debugDraw.SetDrawScale(worldScale);
    debugDraw.SetFlags(b2DebugDraw.e_shapeBit);
    debugDraw.SetFillAlpha(0.5);
    world.SetDebugDraw(debugDraw);
}
```

2. Then, as we need to create a lot of bricks, a function to create a brick starting from its position and size is strongly recommended, so here is a `brick` function with its arguments: brick horizontal and vertical origin, width, and height.

```
private function brick(pX:int,pY:int,w:Number,h:Number):void {
    var bodyDef:b2BodyDef=new b2BodyDef();
    bodyDef.position.Set(pX/worldScale,pY/worldScale);
    // bodyDef.type=b2Body.b2_dynamicBody;
    var polygonShape:b2PolygonShape=new b2PolygonShape();
    polygonShape.SetAsBox(w/2/worldScale,h/2/worldScale);
    var fixtureDef:b2FixtureDef=new b2FixtureDef();
    fixtureDef.shape=polygonShape;
    fixtureDef.density=2;
    fixtureDef.restitution=0.4;
    fixtureDef.friction=0.5;
    var theBrick:b2Body=world.CreateBody(bodyDef);
    theBrick.CreateFixture(fixtureDef);
}
```

> Obviously, if you want you can also pass as arguments the density, friction, and restitution.

If you look at the code, there's nothing new, but I want you to have a look at the highlighted lines:

- First, the line that sets the `type` attribute is commented, so at the moment we will create static bodies. When you are designing a level, it is better to start with static bodies, and once you are satisfied, turn them into dynamic bodies. Static bodies will help you to see the exact location of each body, avoiding overlapping or other design mistakes.

- Second, in the `SetAsBox` attributes, the width and the height of the brick are divided by two before they get divided by `worldScale` too. I am doing this because I want to call the `brick` function with real width and height in pixels, no matter if the `SetAsBox` method wants the half-width and the half-height as you already know.

Adding Bodies to the World

3. The following is how the functions in your `Main` class will look now:

```
public function Main() {
  world=new b2World(new b2Vec2(0,5),true);
  debugDraw();
  // level design goes here
  addEventListener(Event.ENTER_FRAME,updateWorld);
}
private function brick(pX:int,pY:int,w:Number,h:Number):void {
  var bodyDef:b2BodyDef=new b2BodyDef();
  bodyDef.position.Set(pX/worldScale,pY/worldScale);
  //bodyDef.type=b2Body.b2_dynamicBody;
  var polygonShape:b2PolygonShape=new b2PolygonShape();
  polygonShape.SetAsBox(w/2/worldScale,h/2/worldScale);
  var fixtureDef:b2FixtureDef=new b2FixtureDef();
  fixtureDef.shape=polygonShape;
  fixtureDef.density=2;
  fixtureDef.restitution=0.4;
  fixtureDef.friction=0.5;
  var theBrick:b2Body=world.CreateBody(bodyDef);
  theBrick.CreateFixture(fixtureDef);
}
private function debugDraw():void {
  var debugDraw:b2DebugDraw=new b2DebugDraw();
  var debugSprite:Sprite=new Sprite();
  addChild(debugSprite);
  debugDraw.SetSprite(debugSprite);
  debugDraw.SetDrawScale(worldScale);
  debugDraw.SetFlags(b2DebugDraw.e_shapeBit);
  debugDraw.SetFillAlpha(0.5);
  world.SetDebugDraw(debugDraw);
}
private function updateWorld(e:Event):void {
  world.Step(1/30,10,10);
  world.ClearForces();
  world.DrawDebugData();
}
```

Now the `Main` function is simple and clear, and we can build our level just by calling the `brick` function six times, one per block.

Also, notice how I have set the gravity to `(0,5)` rather than real-world gravity as in the falling ball example. A weaker gravity will make the totem destroy and fall down slowly, with a dramatic effect. Anyway, it's just a game-design choice, and you're free to set your own gravity.

4. Let's get back to our `Main` function now:

```
public function Main() {
   world=new b2World(new b2Vec2(0,5),true);
   debugDraw();
   brick(275,435,30,30);
   brick(365,435,30,30);
   brick(320,405,120,30);
   brick(320,375,60,30);
   brick(305,345,90,30);
   brick(320,300,120,60);
   addEventListener(Event.ENTER_FRAME,updateWorld);
}
```

From the first to the last `brick` call, we have built the left basement, the right basement, and then the remaining bricks from bottom to top, respectively.

5. Test your movie.

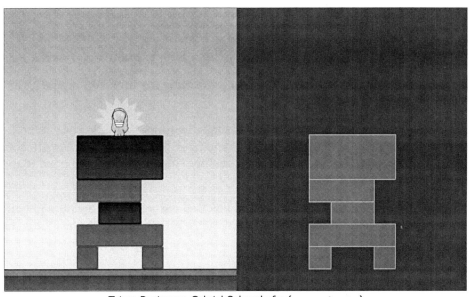

Totem Destroyer: Gabriel Ochsenhofer (www.gabs.tv)

I think you should be quite happy with it, as you have learned to build your first totem, ready to host the idol on top of it.

Before we add the floor and make the totem dynamic, I want you to think about the idol.

What if we want the idol to have a shape that is different than boxes and circles?

Adding Bodies to the World

Creating compound bodies

The idol is the main character in Totem Destroyer, we can't represent it with just a box, or the curse of the totem will persecute us forever.

I was thinking about something like the following figure:

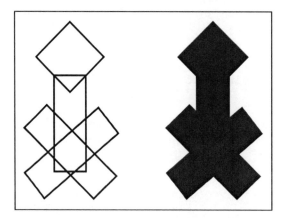

This is what I call an idol, and this is what we are going to build with Box2D.

On the left-hand side, the outline of the bodies forming the idol, and on the right-hand side the finished idol silhouette.

The first thing you can see is that the idol is made by more than one body joined together to create a single, complex body. Remember Box2D only works with convex polygons. Unlike totem bricks, which are just single boxes stacked, we need to merge all the idol objects in some way.

Easy things first. We'll start with the vertical box that we already know how to build, and we are going to build it in the `Main` function just after building the last totem brick.

```
public function Main() {
  world=new b2World(new b2Vec2(0,5),true);
  debugDraw();
  brick(275,435,30,30);
  brick(365,435,30,30);
  brick(320,405,120,30);
  brick(320,375,60,30);
  brick(305,345,90,30);
  brick(320,300,120,60);
  idol(320,242);
  addEventListener(Event.ENTER_FRAME,updateWorld);
}
```

Where `idol` is the function in which we are going to build the idol:

```
private function idol(pX:Number,pY:Number):void {
    var bodyDef:b2BodyDef=new b2BodyDef();
    bodyDef.position.Set(pX/worldScale,pY/worldScale);
    var polygonShape:b2PolygonShape=new b2PolygonShape();
    polygonShape.SetAsBox(5/worldScale,20/worldScale);
    var fixtureDef:b2FixtureDef=new b2FixtureDef();
    fixtureDef.shape=polygonShape;
    fixtureDef.density=1;
    fixtureDef.restitution=0.4;
    fixtureDef.friction=0.5;
    var theIdol:b2Body=world.CreateBody(bodyDef);
    theIdol.CreateFixture(fixtureDef);
}
```

At the moment we have just added another box shape, like the ones used for the bricks, so there's no need to explain the code.

Test the movie and you'll see the body of the idol.

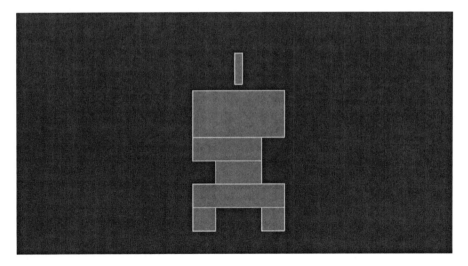

The second part of the idol we are going to create is the cross at its base. The cross itself is formed by two box shapes just like the ones you are used to, but this time they are rotated by 45 degrees clockwise and counterclockwise.

The creation of oriented box shapes is the next thing you will learn.

Creating an oriented box shape

To create an oriented box shape, we will use a `b2PolygonShape` method similar to `SetAsBox`, yet more advanced and called the `SetAsOrientedBox` method.

The arguments are the width and height of the box, the center of the box, also defined as a `b2Vec2` object, and the rotation in radians.

1. Applying this concept, the `idol` function continues in the following way:

    ```
    var bW:Number=5/worldScale;
    var bH:Number=20/worldScale;
    var boxPos:b2Vec2=new b2Vec2(0,10/worldScale);
    var boxAngle:Number=- Math.PI/4;
    ```

    The first two lines are quite understandable as we are defining the size of the box, which is same as the box we just created.

    Looking at the third line, where I define the position, you could have some doubts. The center of the body of the first idol box was (320,242) in pixels, so why am I placing the second idol box at (0,10)? Shouldn't it be placed near to the first idol box?

    That's the magic of compound objects you are about to learn. Now we aren't defining the position as absolute, but as relative to the position of the body of the first idol box.

    So the meaning of the line is: the box will be placed a little below the center of the body.

    The last line just specifies the angle in radians, 45 degrees counterclockwise.

2. With these four variables, you can call the `SetAsOrientedBox` method in the following way:

    ```
    polygonShape.SetAsOrientedBox(bW,bH,boxPos,boxAngle);
    ```

3. Then, as usual, we need to update the fixture shape:

    ```
    fixtureDef.shape=polygonShape;
    ```

4. And now, the magic. Rather than creating a new `b2Body` object, we attach the fixture to the existing `theIdol` body:

    ```
    theIdol.CreateFixture(fixtureDef);
    ```

5. If we apply the same concept for the other box, we need to change the `boxAngle` variable:

    ```
    boxAngle=Math.PI/4;
    ```

Chapter 2

6. Then we can build the oriented box, update fixture shape, and add it to the `theIdol` body:

   ```
   polygonShape.SetAsOrientedBox(bW.bH,boxPos,boxAngle);
   fixtureDef.shape=polygonShape;
   theIdol.CreateFixture(fixtureDef);
   ```

7. And finally, the `idol` function will look like the following code snippet:

   ```
   private function idol(pX:Number,pY:Number):void{
     var bodyDef:b2BodyDef=new b2BodyDef();
     bodyDef.position.Set(pX/worldScale,pY/worldScale);
     var polygonShape:b2PolygonShape=new b2PolygonShape();
     polygonShape.SetAsBox(5/worldScale,20/worldScale);
     var fixtureDef:b2FixtureDef=new b2FixtureDef();
     fixtureDef.shape=polygonShape;
     fixtureDef.density=1;
     fixtureDef.restitution=0.4;
     fixtureDef.friction=0.5;
     var theIdol:b2Body=world.CreateBody(bodyDef);
     theIdol.CreateFixture(fixtureDef);
     var bW:Number=5/worldScale;
     var bH:Number=20/worldScale;
     var boxPos:b2Vec2=new b2Vec2(0,10/worldScale);
     var boxAngle:Number=-Math.PI/4;
     polygonShape.SetAsOrientedBox(bW,bH,boxPos,boxAngle);
     fixtureDef.shape=polygonShape;
     theIdol.CreateFixture(fixtureDef);
     boxAngle=Math.PI/4;
     polygonShape.SetAsOrientedBox(bW,bH,boxPos,boxAngle);
     fixtureDef.shape=polygonShape;
     theIdol.CreateFixture(fixtureDef);
   }
   ```

8. Test the movie to see how the idol now looks similar to our sketch:

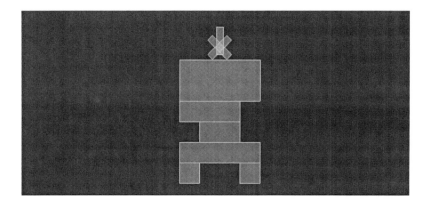

Adding Bodies to the World

Now, we still need to build its head.

At this time, you should be able to build it by yourself. All in all it's just another oriented box to be part of the compound object. That's why I will show you another way to do it, using the most powerful way to create a polygon shape.

Creating any kind of convex polygons

Box2D allows you to create any kind of polygon shape, as long as the polygon is **convex**, which means it must have all interior angles less than 180 degrees, so all the vertices point away from the center, and you provide its vertices in *clockwise* order.

1. First, let's create a vector to store all vertices:

    ```
    var vertices:Vector.<b2Vec2>=new Vector.<b2Vec2>();
    ```

2. Then we will push all vertices in clockwise order, as `b2Vec2` objects, specifying the relative position of the vertices to the center of the idol body.

    ```
    vertices.push(new b2Vec2(-15/worldScale,-25/worldScale));
    vertices.push(new b2Vec2(0,-40/worldScale));
    vertices.push(new b2Vec2(15/worldScale,-25/worldScale));
    vertices.push(new b2Vec2(0,-10/worldScale));
    ```

3. The previous lines of code are the four vertices of idol's head. Now let's turn this vector into a polygon shape:

    ```
    polygonShape.SetAsVector(vertices,4);
    ```

    The `SetAsVector` method turns any vector of clockwise vertices into a polygon shape. The second argument just represents the number of vertices to consider.

4. Finally, as usual, you need to update the fixture shape and add it to the `theIdol` body:

    ```
    fixtureDef.shape=polygonShape;
    theIdol.CreateFixture(fixtureDef);
    ```

5. The following is how the `idol` function looks now:

    ```
    private function idol(pX:Number,pY:Number):void{
      var bodyDef:b2BodyDef=new b2BodyDef();
      bodyDef.position.Set(pX/worldScale,pY/worldScale);
      var polygonShape:b2PolygonShape=new b2PolygonShape();
      polygonShape.SetAsBox(5/worldScale,20/worldScale);
      var fixtureDef:b2FixtureDef=new b2FixtureDef();
      fixtureDef.shape=polygonShape;
      fixtureDef.density=1;
    ```

Chapter 2

```
fixtureDef.restitution=0.4;
fixtureDef.friction=0.5;
var theIdol:b2Body=world.CreateBody(bodyDef);
theIdol.CreateFixture(fixtureDef);
var bW:Number=5/worldScale;
var bH:Number=20/worldScale;
var boxPos:b2Vec2=new b2Vec2(0,10/worldScale);
var boxAngle:Number=-Math.PI/4;
polygonShape.SetAsOrientedBox(bW,bH,boxPos,boxAngle);
fixtureDef.shape=polygonShape;
theIdol.CreateFixture(fixtureDef);
boxAngle=Math.PI/4;
polygonShape.SetAsOrientedBox(bW,bH,boxPos,boxAngle);
fixtureDef.shape=polygonShape;
theIdol.CreateFixture(fixtureDef);
var vertices:Vector.<b2Vec2>=new Vector.<b2Vec2>();
vertices.push(new b2Vec2(-15/worldScale,
  -25/worldScale));
vertices.push(new b2Vec2(0,-40/worldScale));
vertices.push(new b2Vec2(15/worldScale,
  -25/worldScale));
vertices.push(new b2Vec2(0,-10/worldScale));
polygonShape.SetAsVector(vertices,4);
fixtureDef.shape=polygonShape;
theIdol.CreateFixture(fixtureDef);
}
```

6. Test the movie and you'll finally see your complete idol on the top of the totem:

Adding Bodies to the World

7. At this time you just need to create the floor, which is a static box (shown with a function):

    ```
    public function Main() {
      world=new b2World(new b2Vec2(0,5),true);
      debugDraw();
      brick(275,435,30,30);
      brick(365,435,30,30);
      brick(320,405,120,30);
      brick(320,375,60,30);
      brick(305,345,90,30);
      brick(320,300,120,60);
      idol(320,242);
      floor();
      addEventListener(Event.ENTER_FRAME,updateWorld);
    }
    ```

8. Where the `floor` function is defined as follows:

    ```
    private function floor():void {
      var bodyDef:b2BodyDef=new b2BodyDef();
      bodyDef.position.Set(320/worldScale,465/worldScale);
      var polygonShape:b2PolygonShape=new b2PolygonShape();
      polygonShape.SetAsBox(320/worldScale,15/worldScale);
      var fixtureDef:b2FixtureDef=new b2FixtureDef();
      fixtureDef.shape=polygonShape;
      fixtureDef.restitution=0.4;
      fixtureDef.friction=0.5;
      var theFloor:b2Body=world.CreateBody(bodyDef);
      theFloor.CreateFixture(fixtureDef);
    }
    ```

9. Then make the bricks dynamic by removing the commented line:

    ```
    private function
      brick(pX:int,pY:int,w:Number,h:Number):void {
      var bodyDef:b2BodyDef=new b2BodyDef();
      bodyDef.position.Set(pX/worldScale,pY/worldScale);
      bodyDef.type=b2Body.b2_dynamicBody;
      var polygonShape:b2PolygonShape=new b2PolygonShape();
      polygonShape.SetAsBox(w/2/worldScale,h/2/worldScale);
      var fixtureDef:b2FixtureDef=new b2FixtureDef();
      fixtureDef.shape=polygonShape;
      fixtureDef.density=2;
      fixtureDef.restitution=0.4;
    ```

```
    fixtureDef.friction=0.5;
    var theBrick:b2Body=world.CreateBody(bodyDef);
    theBrick.CreateFixture(fixtureDef);
}
```

10. And finally, we make the idol dynamic too:

    ```
    private function idol(pX:Number,pY:Number):void {
      var bodyDef:b2BodyDef=new b2BodyDef();
      bodyDef.position.Set(pX/worldScale,pY/worldScale);
      bodyDef.type=b2Body.b2_dynamicBody;
      var polygonShape:b2PolygonShape=new b2PolygonShape();
      polygonShape.SetAsBox(5/worldScale,20/worldScale);
      var fixtureDef:b2FixtureDef=new b2FixtureDef();
      fixtureDef.shape=polygonShape;
      fixtureDef.density=1;
      fixtureDef.restitution=0.4;
      fixtureDef.friction=0.5;
      var theIdol:b2Body=world.CreateBody(bodyDef);
      theIdol.CreateFixture(fixtureDef);
      var bW:Number=5/worldScale;
      var bH:Number=20/worldScale;
      var boxPos:b2Vec2=new b2Vec2(0,10/worldScale);
      var boxAngle:Number=- Math.PI/4;
      polygonShape.SetAsOrientedBox(bW,bH,boxPos,boxAngle);
      fixtureDef.shape=polygonShape;
      theIdol.CreateFixture(fixtureDef);
      boxAngle=Math.PI/4;
      polygonShape.SetAsOrientedBox(bW,bH,boxPos,boxAngle);
      fixtureDef.shape=polygonShape;
      theIdol.CreateFixture(fixtureDef);
      var vertices:Vector.<b2Vec2>=new Vector.<b2Vec2>();
      vertices.push(new b2Vec2(-15/worldScale,
        -25/worldScale));
      vertices.push(new b2Vec2(0,-40/worldScale));
      vertices.push(new b2Vec2(15/worldScale,
        -25/worldScale));
      vertices.push(new b2Vec2(0,-10/worldScale));
      polygonShape.SetAsVector(vertices,4);
      fixtureDef.shape=polygonShape;
      theIdol.CreateFixture(fixtureDef);
    }
    ```

As said at the beginning of the chapter, your journey into Box2D bodies ends with the creation of a real Totem Destroyer level.

This is where this chapter ends, but you are going to learn how to do a lot of new things to the totem in the next chapter.

Summary

This was one of the most important chapters of the book as you just learned how to create bodies and used them to design levels of successful games, such as Totem Destroyer.

To get used to Box2D bodies, I would suggest you create more Totem Destroyer levels or some Red Remover or Angry Birds levels. All in all, it's just a matter of shapes.

3
Interacting with Bodies

Every Box2D based game has its own way to interact with bodies. Totem Destroyer and Red Remover allow the player to destroy bodies by clicking them with the mouse, while Angry Birds makes bodies (birds) fly by dragging them. You already know how to create primitive and complex bodies; it's time to see how Box2D allows us to interact with bodies in its world.

In this chapter you will learn various ways to interact with and get information from Box2D bodies, including:

- Selecting bodies with the mouse
- Destroying bodies
- Setting custom properties to bodies
- Looping through all bodies in the world
- Getting body information

By the end of the chapter, you will have a completely playable Totem Destroyer level.

The simplest and most intuitive way by which we can interact with Box2D bodies is destroying them with a mouse click.

Interacting with Bodies

Selecting and destroying bodies with a mouse click

We need to complete the Totem Destroyer prototype, so these concepts will be applied to the script you made in *Chapter 2, Adding Bodies to the World*. You should have a totem ready to be destroyed with an idol on top of it.

1. Before we see how to select and destroy bodies, we need to add a mouse click listener, so we need to import a new class to handle mouse events in our Main class:

   ```
   import flash.display.Sprite;
   import flash.events.Event;
   import flash.events.MouseEvent;
   import Box2D.Dynamics.*;
   import Box2D.Collision.*;
   import Box2D.Collision.Shapes.*;
   import Box2D.Common.Math.*;
   ```

2. Then we can add the mouse listener in the Main function:

   ```
   public function Main() {
       world=new b2World(new b2Vec2(0,5),true);
       debugDraw();
       brick(275,435,30,30);
       brick(365,435,30,30);
       brick(320,405,120,30);
       brick(320,375,60,30);
       brick(305,345,90,30);
       brick(320,300,120,60);
       idol(320,242);
       floor();
       addEventListener(Event.ENTER_FRAME,updateWorld);
       stage.addEventListener(MouseEvent.CLICK,destroyBrick);
   }
   ```

   I am not explaining the previous code as it has nothing to do with Box2D, and you should already know how to create a mouse listener.

3. Things start to become interesting in the `destroyBrick` function, which is called at every mouse click:

   ```
   private function destroyBrick(e:MouseEvent):void {
       var pX:Number=mouseX/worldScale;
       var pY:Number=mouseY/worldScale;
       world.QueryPoint(queryCallback,new b2Vec2(pX,pY));
   }
   ```

Let's explain it line by line. The first two lines just convert mouse x and y positions obtained with `mouseX` and `mouseY` respectively from values in pixels to values in meters, according to the `worldScale` variable. This way variables `pX` and `pY` will store world coordinates of the pixel we just clicked.

4. Now it's time to see if there's a body in the point we clicked. The world's `QueryPoint` method queries the world for all fixtures that contain a point, and if a fixture contains the point clicked by the mouse, then we can say we have clicked such a fixture.

   Let's have a look at its arguments; first, a callback function we called `queryCallback`, then the coordinates of the point we want to check expressed as a `b2Vec2` object, which represents translated mouse coordinates.

   The `queryCallback` function is the core of this script and will take as argument the fixture that contains the point, if any. As there could be more than one fixture on the same point (think about overlapping static bodies), you can make `queryCallback` return `true` if you want it to check for the next fixture, or false to stop checking.

   At the moment we assume there can be only one fixture under the mouse, so I would write the `queryCallBack` function in the following way:

   ```
   private function queryCallback(fixture:b2Fixture):Boolean {
     trace(fixture);
     return false;
   }
   ```

   At the moment we just want to generate some debug text in the output window, so once you test the movie and click on a body, you'll see the following text:

   > **[object b2Fixture]**

   This means we have successfully executed the `queryCallback` function, and we can determine the fixture that the player clicked on, if any.

5. Unfortunately, just knowing the fixture is not enough, as we also need to know the body we are going to remove. To get a body starting from a fixture, you can use the `GetBody` method, so you can make the following changes to the `queryCallBack` function:

   ```
   private function queryCallback(fixture:b2Fixture):Boolean {
     var touchedBody:b2Body=fixture.GetBody();
     trace(touchedBody);
     return false;
   }
   ```

Interacting with Bodies

If you test the movie now and then click on a body, you'll see the following text in the output window:

[object b2Body]

Now we know which body the player clicked on, it's time to destroy it for real. To remove a body from the world, use the world's `DestroyBody` method and finally you are able to smash the totem.

```
private function queryCallback(fixture:b2Fixture):Boolean {
  var touchedBody:b2Body=fixture.GetBody();
  world.DestroyBody(touchedBody);
  return false;
}
```

6. Test the movie. Click on a brick and you will see it disappear, destroying the totem:

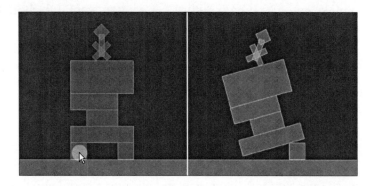

Anyway, we still have a problem. In Totem Destroyer, not all of the bricks can be destroyed, but at the moment if you click on any of them, you will destroy it.

Moreover, you can even destroy the idol and the ground itself.

Look at the previous screenshot. On the left, I destroyed the floor, which is wrong. On the right, I destroyed the upper big brick, which can't be destroyed in the original game.

That's quite an issue, so we must find a way to tell Box2D which bodies can be destroyed and which bodies cannot.

Luckily, Box2D body definition management is so advanced that we can even add our custom attributes to a body.

Assigning custom attributes to bodies

Custom attributes can be of any type, but at the moment we'll just add a string: `breakable` for breakable bricks, and `unbreakable` for unbreakable bricks.

1. First, we'll be passing the string as an argument of the `brick` function, so to reproduce the first level of Totem Destroyer we'll modify the `Main` function in the following way:

   ```
   public function Main() {
     world=new b2World(new b2Vec2(0,5),true);
     debugDraw();
     brick(275,435,30,30,"breakable");
     brick(365,435,30,30,"breakable");
     brick(320,405,120,30,"breakable");
     brick(320,375,60,30,"unbreakable");
     brick(305,345,90,30,"breakable");
     brick(320,300,120,60,"unbreakable");
     idol(320,242);
     floor();
     addEventListener(Event.ENTER_FRAME,updateWorld);
     stage.addEventListener(MouseEvent.CLICK,destroyBrick);
   }
   ```

2. And now let's have a look at how the `brick` function changes:

   ```
   private function
   brick(pX:int,pY:int,w:Number,h:Number,s:String):void {
     var bodyDef:b2BodyDef=new b2BodyDef();
     bodyDef.position.Set(pX/worldScale,pY/worldScale);
     bodyDef.type=b2Body.b2_dynamicBody;
     bodyDef.userData=s;
     var polygonShape:b2PolygonShape=new b2PolygonShape();
     polygonShape.SetAsBox(w/2/worldScale,h/2/worldScale);
     var fixtureDef:b2FixtureDef=new b2FixtureDef();
   ```

Interacting with Bodies

```
    fixtureDef.shape=polygonShape;
    fixtureDef.density=2;
    fixtureDef.restitution=0.4;
    fixtureDef.friction=0.5;
    var theBrick:b2Body=world.CreateBody(bodyDef);
    theBrick.CreateFixture(fixtureDef);
}
```

The string argument is called s and, as you can see when I created the body definition, the userData property stores the string. Remember this property as you will need it in most of your projects, whenever you have to store a specific body data.

When we execute the queryCallback function after our bodies have their data, we need to look for breakable string in our body user data.

We will destroy the body only if we find breakable, and optionally we can output a message when we find unbreakable, such as "you can't destroy this brick". But I am leaving this to you, as I just want to destroy the bricks.

3. Change the queryCallback function in the following way:

```
private function queryCallback(fixture:b2Fixture):Boolean {
    var touchedBody:b2Body=fixture.GetBody();
    var userData:String=touchedBody.GetUserData();
    if (userData=="breakable") {
      world.DestroyBody(touchedBody);
    }
    return false;
}
```

You can read a body user data with the GetUserData method, so we just need to check if we have found the breakable value.

4. Test the movie and you will see you are only able to destroy breakable bricks:

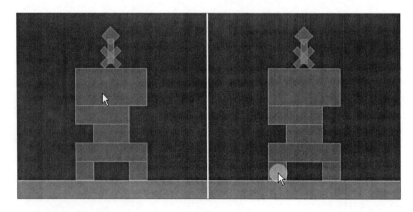

[46]

In the previous screenshot, the big brick cannot be destroyed if you click on it, while the left totem "foot" can be destroyed. It's all a matter of storing and retrieving the right data.

Anyway, setting and getting body user data is not the only way we have to check information about our bodies.

At any time, we can scan through all bodies in the world and get their position and rotation, as well as its speed and other useful information.

Looping through bodies and getting their properties

The next example will build some kind of information display that monitors the idol. At every frame, we'll read the idol position, rotation, and speed. This way, you can assign events according to idol properties, such as giving a bonus if the idol did not fall down, or if it never reached a certain y-speed, or if it moved too far on the left, and so on. Knowing body properties is also very useful when you want to skin your game, as you can synchronize custom graphic assets to what happens in the Box2D World.

One step at time, let's start with our idol monitor. We are going to display idol data in a dynamic text field, so we need to make some basic changes to our class. I won't explain such changes as they are simple AS3 routines you should already know.

1. First, we import the required classes to dynamically generate a text field and give it some style:

    ```
    import flash.display.Sprite;
    import flash.events.Event;
    import flash.events.MouseEvent;
    import flash.text.TextField;
    import flash.text.TextFormat;
    import Box2D.Dynamics.*;
    import Box2D.Collision.*;
    import Box2D.Collision.Shapes.*;
    import Box2D.Common.Math.*;
    ```

2. Then, a couple of new class level variables are added. `textMon` is the text field itself, while `textFormat` is a `TextFormat` variable that will help us to make the text field look prettier.

    ```
    private var world:b2World;
    private var worldScale:Number=30;
    private var textMon:TextField = new TextField();
    var textFormat:TextFormat = new TextFormat();
    ```

Interacting with Bodies

3. Finally, in the `Main` function we add and stylize the text monitor field. Something very basic and easy, just a big white text, as this is out of the scope of this chapter.

```
public function Main() {
  world=new b2World(new b2Vec2(0,5),true);
  debugDraw();
  addChild(textMon);
  textMon.textColor=0xffffff;
  textMon.width=300;
  textMon.height=300;
  textFormat.size=25;
  textMon.defaultTextFormat=textFormat;
  brick(275,435,30,30,"breakable");
  brick(365,435,30,30,"breakable");
  brick(320,405,120,30,"breakable");
  brick(320,375,60,30,"unbreakable");
  brick(305,345,90,30,"breakable");
  brick(320,300,120,60,"unbreakable");
  idol(320,242);
  floor();
  addEventListener(Event.ENTER_FRAME,updateWorld);
  stage.addEventListener(MouseEvent.CLICK,destroyBrick);
}
```

Back to serious things now, we need to somehow identify the idol. One approach uses the `userData` property that we just looked at.

4. So we are adding it just like we made with the bricks. This time we'll be using `idol` rather than `breakable` or `unbreakable`.

```
private function idol(pX:Number,pY:Number):void {
  var bodyDef:b2BodyDef=new b2BodyDef();
  bodyDef.position.Set(pX/worldScale,pY/worldScale);
  bodyDef.type=b2Body.b2_dynamicBody;
  bodyDef.userData="idol";
  var polygonShape:b2PolygonShape=new b2PolygonShape();
  polygonShape.SetAsBox(5/worldScale,20/worldScale);
  var fixtureDef:b2FixtureDef=new b2FixtureDef();
  fixtureDef.shape=polygonShape;
  fixtureDef.density=1;
  fixtureDef.restitution=0.4;
  fixtureDef.friction=0.5;
  var theIdol:b2Body=world.CreateBody(bodyDef);
  theIdol.CreateFixture(fixtureDef);
  var bW:Number=5/worldScale;
```

```
    var bH:Number=20/worldScale;
    var boxPos:b2Vec2=new b2Vec2(0,10/worldScale);
    var boxAngle:Number=- Math.PI/4;
    polygonShape.SetAsOrientedBox(bW,bH,boxPos,boxAngle);
    fixtureDef.shape=polygonShape;
    theIdol.CreateFixture(fixtureDef);
    boxAngle=Math.PI/4;
    polygonShape.SetAsOrientedBox(bW,bH,boxPos,boxAngle);
    fixtureDef.shape=polygonShape;
    theIdol.CreateFixture(fixtureDef);
    var vertices:Vector.<b2Vec2>=new Vector.<b2Vec2>();
    vertices.push(new b2Vec2(-15/worldScale,
      -25/worldScale));
    vertices.push(new b2Vec2(0,-40/worldScale));
    vertices.push(new b2Vec2(15/worldScale,
      -25/worldScale));
    vertices.push(new b2Vec2(0,-10/worldScale));
    polygonShape.SetAsVector(vertices,4);
    fixtureDef.shape=polygonShape;
    theIdol.CreateFixture(fixtureDef);
}
```

5. And now, the core of the script, the code we'll insert into the updateWorld function:

```
private function updateWorld(e:Event):void {
  var radToDeg:Number=180/Math.PI;
  world.Step(1/30,10,10);
  world.ClearForces();
  for (var b:b2Body=world.GetBodyList();
   b; b=b.GetNext()) {
    if (b.GetUserData()=="idol") {
      var position:b2Vec2=b.GetPosition();
      var xPos:Number=Math.round(position.x*worldScale);
      textMon.text=xPos.toString();
      textMon.appendText(",");
      var yPos:Number=Math.round(position.y*worldScale);
      textMon.appendText(yPos.toString());
      textMon.appendText("\nangle: ");
      var angle:Number=
      Math.round(b.GetAngle()*radToDeg);
      textMon.appendText(angle.toString());
      textMon.appendText("\nVelocity: ");
      var velocity:b2Vec2=b.GetLinearVelocity();
      var xVel:Number=Math.round(velocity.x*worldScale);
```

Interacting with Bodies

```
            textMon.appendText(xVel.toString());
            textMon.appendText(",");
            var yVel:Number=Math.round(velocity.y*worldScale);
            textMon.appendText(yVel.toString());
        }
    }
    world.DrawDebugData();
}
```

That's a lot of new code, anyway don't be scared as most of the code is used just to update the text field.

Let's focus on the for loop first. The `GetBodyList` method gets the world body list and returns the first body. You can get the next body with `GetNext` and `GetBodyList` returns `null` if you are at the end of the list. So the three parameters of the for loop can be read in the following way:

- `var b:b2Body=world.GetBodyList()` declares a `b2Body` variable called `b` and assigns it the value of the first body in the world body list.
- `b` is the exit condition, so we'll keep looping until `b` exists, that is, `b` is not `null`, which means we are dealing with a body and we aren't at the end of the list.
- `b=b.GetNext())` gets the next body, it's very similar to an `i++` in a for loop, where `i` goes from `1` to `n>1`.

Now inside the for loop we have a `b` variable representing the current body. Let's see what to do with it. First, we need to know we are dealing with the idol, so we are going to check its user data:

`if (b.GetUserData()=="idol") { /* rest of the code */ }`

Once we know we are working with the idol, let's get its position:

`var position:b2Vec2=b.GetPosition();`

The `GetPosition` method returns the body's origin position as a `b2Vec2` object. If we want to know the position in pixels, we have to convert meters to pixels as you are already used to doing it by now:

```
var xPos:Number=Math.round(position.x*worldScale);
var yPos:Number=Math.round(position.y*worldScale);
```

The previous lines of code perform this task. Now let's see idol rotation.

```
var angle:Number=Math.round(b.GetAngle()*radToDeg);
```

The `GetAngle` method gets the angle of the body in radians. As I am sure you feel more comfortable working with degrees, I converted radians to degrees by multiplying `GetAngle` returned number by a variable called `radToDeg`, which is defined on the first line of the `updateWorld` function.

To get degrees from radians, use the following formula:

*Degrees = Radians * 180 / PI*

To get radians from degrees, use the inverse:

*Radians = Degrees * PI / 180*

There is a lot of additional data we can get from the idol, but at the moment let's just get some other information, the velocity.

```
var velocity:b2Vec2=b.GetLinearVelocity();
```

The `GetLinearVelocity` method gets the linear velocity of the center of the mass and returns it in a `b2Vec2` object representing the horizontal and vertical speed in meters per second.

As we still want to work with pixels, another conversion is needed:

```
var xVel:Number=Math.round(velocity.x*worldScale);
var yVel:Number=Math.round(velocity.y*worldScale);
```

The remaining lines just manage the output on the text field.

Interacting with Bodies

6. Test the movie and make something to move the idol, and you'll see the idol monitor updating with idol data in real time:

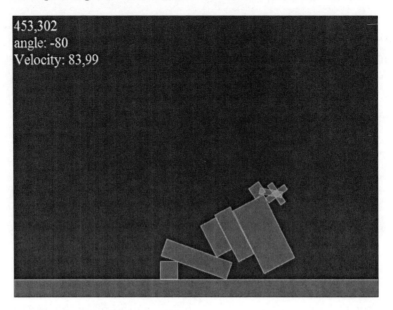

That's enough with body interaction at the moment; I don't want to give you an overload of information because there's still a lot to explain before you'll find advanced body interaction really useful.

By the way, now you have learned how to destroy bricks (and only given bricks) with the click of the mouse, and to track idol position and angle.

Summary

Now you know how to select and destroy a body, as well as get body information. With these concepts you can build a complete, though not that advanced, Totem Destroyer prototype.

Although you aren't able to determine if the idol touched the ground (failing the level), you can check for its angle to be between -30 and +30 to show that the idol did not fall down, and create your first Totem Destroyer game.

4
Applying Forces to Bodies

Box2D world is ruled by forces and is able to apply them to bodies to give us a realistic simulation, but if you couldn't manually apply forces to bodies, you won't be able to move bodies, fire bullets, throw birds, drive cars, and do all the awesome things you see when you play physics games.

In this chapter you will learn how to apply forces to move bodies in different ways, managing a lot of new Box2D features including:

- Applying a force to a body
- Applying an impulse to a body
- Setting the linear velocity to a body
- Knowing the mass of a body
- Applying the right kind of force according to your gameplay needs
- Mixing physics with non-physics assets in your game

By the end of the chapter, you will be able to create an Angry Birds level, sling included.

Falling apples, revamped

The legend says Newton discovered the gravity after being hit by a falling apple. You will learn forces by raising some objects from the ground.

We'll start with a basic script that will place three dynamic spheres on a static floor.

The following will be your starting `Main` class:

```
package {
    import flash.display.Sprite;
    import flash.events.Event;
```

```
import Box2D.Dynamics.*;
import Box2D.Collision.*;
import Box2D.Collision.Shapes.*;
import Box2D.Common.Math.*;
public class Main extends Sprite {
   private var world:b2World;
   private var worldScale:Number=30;
   private var sphereVector:Vector.<b2Body>;
   public function Main() {
      world=new b2World(new b2Vec2(0,10),true);
      debugDraw();
      floor();
      sphereVector=new Vector.<b2Body>();
      for (var i:int=0; i<3; i++) {
         sphereVector.push(sphere(170+i*150,410,40));
      }
      addEventListener(Event.ENTER_FRAME,updateWorld);
   }
   private function sphere(pX:int,pY:int,r:Number):b2Body {
      var bodyDef:b2BodyDef=new b2BodyDef();
      bodyDef.position.Set(pX/worldScale,pY/worldScale);
      bodyDef.type=b2Body.b2_dynamicBody;
      var circleShape:b2CircleShape
      circleShape=new b2CircleShape(r/worldScale);
      var fixtureDef:b2FixtureDef=new b2FixtureDef();
      fixtureDef.shape=circleShape;
      fixtureDef.density=2;
      fixtureDef.restitution=0.4;
      fixtureDef.friction=0.5;
      var theSphere:b2Body=world.CreateBody(bodyDef);
      theSphere.CreateFixture(fixtureDef);
      return theSphere;
   }
   private function floor():void {
      var bodyDef:b2BodyDef=new b2BodyDef();
      bodyDef.position.Set(320/worldScale,465/worldScale);
      var polygonShape:b2PolygonShape=new b2PolygonShape();
      polygonShape.SetAsBox(320/worldScale,15/worldScale);
      var fixtureDef:b2FixtureDef=new b2FixtureDef();
      fixtureDef.shape=polygonShape;
      fixtureDef.restitution=0.4;
      fixtureDef.friction=0.5;
      var theFloor:b2Body=world.CreateBody(bodyDef);
      theFloor.CreateFixture(fixtureDef);
```

```
        }
        private function debugDraw():void {
            var debugDraw:b2DebugDraw=new b2DebugDraw();
            var debugSprite:Sprite=new Sprite();
            addChild(debugSprite);
            debugDraw.SetSprite(debugSprite);
            debugDraw.SetDrawScale(worldScale);
            debugDraw.SetFlags(b2DebugDraw.e_shapeBit);
            debugDraw.SetFillAlpha(0.5);
            world.SetDebugDraw(debugDraw);
        }
        private function updateWorld(e:Event):void {
            world.Step(1/30,10,10);
            world.ClearForces();
            world.DrawDebugData();
        }
    }
}
```

You should be familiar with everything in it as it is just a minor modification of the totem script as seen in the previous chapters. updateWorld, floor, and debugDraw functions are exactly the same, while the sphere function creates a dynamic sphere given its center and the radius in pixels.

The only difference is that the sphere function not only creates a sphere, but it also returns its b2Body, which I am inserting in a class-level vector called sphereVector.

Test the movie and you'll see three of your spheres lying on the ground:

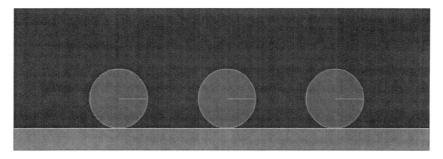

Each sphere is represented by a sphereVector item, from left to right we have sphereVector[0], sphereVector[1], and sphereVector[2].

It's time to make them jump. There are three dynamic bodies in this example because you are about to learn three different ways to apply forces to bodies, each with its pros and cons.

Applying Forces to Bodies

Force, impulse, and linear velocity

Let's jump straight to the point with some new lines in the `Main` function:

```
public function Main() {
  world=new b2World(new b2Vec2(0,10),true);
  debugDraw();
  floor();
  sphereVector=new Vector.<b2Body>();
  for (var i:int=0; i<3; i++) {
    sphereVector.push(sphere(170+i*150,410,40));
  }
  var force:b2Vec2=new b2Vec2(0,-15);
  var sphereCenter:b2Vec2=sphereVector[0].GetWorldCenter();
  sphereVector[0].ApplyForce(force,sphereCenter);
  sphereCenter=sphereVector[1].GetWorldCenter();
  sphereVector[1].ApplyImpulse(force,sphereCenter);
  sphereVector[2].SetLinearVelocity(force);
  addEventListener(Event.ENTER_FRAME,updateWorld);
}
```

This is the core of this chapter and it's a lot of new stuff, so let's look at it line by line:

```
var force:b2Vec2=new b2Vec2(0,-15);
```

First, we need to create a `b2Vec2` variable that will represent the force we want to apply to all spheres. Setting it at `(0,-15)` means this is a vertical force, which should make the spheres jump.

Having a force is not enough if we don't have a point at which to apply the force. In this case, we want the force to be applied to the center of the mass of each sphere.

```
var sphereCenter:b2Vec2=sphereVector[0].GetWorldCenter();
```

To determine the center of the mass of a body, we can use the `GetWorldCenter` method of `b2Body`. It returns a `b2Vec2` object with the center of the mass.

In this case, the `sphereCenter` variable will contain the center of the left sphere.

```
sphereVector[0].ApplyForce(force,sphereCenter);
```

The previous line of code shows the first way to apply a force to a body. The `ApplyForce` method applies a force at a point, usually in newton. If the force is not applied at the center of the mass, it will generate a torque and affect the angular velocity, and that's why we wanted to know the center of the mass. The `ApplyForce` method also wakes up the body, if it is in the inactive sleep state.

```
sphereCenter=sphereVector[1].GetWorldCenter();
```

Once we have applied the force on the left sphere, let's move on to the middle one. We determine its center just like before, and then it's time to add another kind of force.

```
sphereVector[1].ApplyImpulse(force,sphereCenter);
```

The `ApplyImpulse` method applies an impulse at a point, usually in newton-second, immediately modifying its velocity. It also modifies the angular velocity if the point of application is not at the center of the mass, which is not in this case, and wakes up the body.

Now that we are done with the middle sphere, let's see the right sphere:

```
sphereVector[2].SetLinearVelocity(force);
```

The `SetLinearVelocity` method sets the linear velocity of the center of the mass. It does not need a second argument such as `ApplyForce` and `ApplyImpulse` as it's always working in the center of the mass.

Are you wondering how the spheres will react to these forces? We need to add some code to measure what's going on with them, so first we are going to store sphere's vertical position into the `userData` property in the `sphere` function:

```
private function sphere(pX:int,pY:int,r:Number):b2Body {
  var bodyDef:b2BodyDef=new b2BodyDef();
  bodyDef.position.Set(pX/worldScale,pY/worldScale);
  bodyDef.type=b2Body.b2_dynamicBody;
  bodyDef.userData=pY;
  var circleShape:b2CircleShape;
  circleShape=new b2CircleShape(r/worldScale);
  var fixtureDef:b2FixtureDef=new b2FixtureDef();
  fixtureDef.shape=circleShape;
  fixtureDef.density=2;
  fixtureDef.restitution=0.4;
  fixtureDef.friction=0.5;
  var theSphere:b2Body=world.CreateBody(bodyDef);
  theSphere.CreateFixture(fixtureDef);
  return theSphere;
}
```

There's no need to say how versatile and what a lifesaver `userData` is when we need to store custom information of a body.

Now, it's time to print some text in the output window, changing `updateWorld` in the following way:

```
private function updateWorld(e:Event):void {
  var maxHeight:Number;
  var currHeight:Number;
```

```
        var outHeight:Number;
        world.Step(1/30,10,10);
        for (var i:int=0; i<3; i++) {
           maxHeight=sphereVector[i].GetUserData();
           currHeight=sphereVector[i].GetPosition().y*worldScale;
           maxHeight=Math.min(maxHeight,currHeight);
           sphereVector[i].SetUserData(maxHeight);
           outHeight=sphereVector[i].GetUserData();
           trace("Sphere "+i+":"+Math.round(outHeight));
        }
        trace("---------------");
        world.ClearForces();
        world.DrawDebugData();
     }
```

We want to keep track of the maximum height reached by each sphere, so we are looking for the minimum value of y position in pixels of each sphere.

The changes that we saw just update the `userData` property with the minimum value between `userData` itself that represent the highest y position tracked so far and the current y position, and then print the result on the output window.

Test the movie and you will see the rightmost sphere doing a high jump, while the remaining spheres seem to remain on the ground:

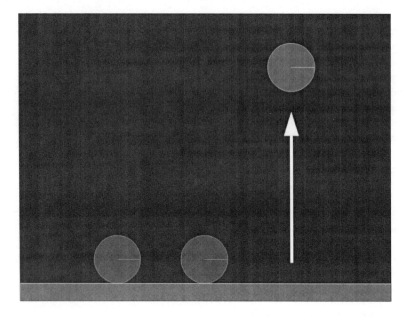

Also, looking at the text in the output window confirms what we saw in the movie. The rightmost sphere reached pixel 80, moving up by 330 pixels, the middle sphere moved by only 2 pixels, and the leftmost sphere did not move at all.

- **Sphere 0:410**
- **Sphere 1:408**
- **Sphere 2:80**

Ok, let's say probably the spheres are too heavy to react to the forces (but remember the rightmost sphere jumped quite high), so we are reducing their density from 2 to 1 in the sphere function:

```
private function sphere(pX:int,pY:int,r:Number):b2Body {
   var bodyDef:b2BodyDef=new b2BodyDef();
   bodyDef.position.Set(pX/worldScale,pY/worldScale);
   bodyDef.type=b2Body.b2_dynamicBody;
   bodyDef.userData=pY;
   var circleShape:b2CircleShape;
   circleShape=new b2CircleShape(r/worldScale);
   var fixtureDef:b2FixtureDef=new b2FixtureDef();
   fixtureDef.shape=circleShape;
   fixtureDef.density=1;
   fixtureDef.restitution=0.4;
   fixtureDef.friction=0.5;
   var theSphere:b2Body=world.CreateBody(bodyDef);
   theSphere.CreateFixture(fixtureDef);
   return theSphere;
}
```

Let's test the movie again and see what happens:

- **Sphere 0:410**
- **Sphere 1:401**
- **Sphere 2:80**

The first thing which should come to your notice is that the rightmost sphere reached exactly the same height as before, no matter if the density changed.

That's because `SetLinearVelocity` just sets the linear velocity of a body, no matter of its mass or previous velocity. It just sets the velocity. Full stop!

On the other hand, the middle sphere jumped a bit more than before, so this means `ApplyImpulse` depends on the mass of a body.

Applying an impulse to get a linear velocity

Now, given two sleeping spheres with the same mass and a force to apply, if `SetLinearVelocity` sets the velocity despite the mass and `ApplyImpulse` is affected by the mass, what if we apply to `ApplyImpulse` a force which is "mass" times the force applied to `SetLinearVelocity`, changing the `Main` function in the following way:

```
public function Main() {
  world=new b2World(new b2Vec2(0,10),true);
  debugDraw();
  floor();
  sphereVector=new Vector.<b2Body>();
  for (var i:int=0; i<3; i++) {
    sphereVector.push(sphere(170+i*150,410,40));
  }
  var force:b2Vec2=new b2Vec2(0,-15);
  var forceByMass:b2Vec2=force.Copy();
  forceByMass.Multiply(sphereVector[1].GetMass());
  var sphereCenter:b2Vec2=sphereVector[0].GetWorldCenter();
  sphereVector[0].ApplyForce(force,sphereCenter);
  sphereCenter=sphereVector[1].GetWorldCenter();
  sphereVector[1].ApplyImpulse(forceByMass,sphereCenter);
  sphereVector[2].SetLinearVelocity(force);
  addEventListener(Event.ENTER_FRAME,updateWorld);
}
```

We also have a couple of new concepts. First, look at the `Copy` method, used to copy a `b2Vec2` object to avoid new vector from being handled by reference. Then, the `Multiply` method multiplies a `b2Vec2` object by a given number, which in this case is the mass of the sphere. The `GetMass` method of `b2Body` returns the mass of the body in kilograms. In the end, we defined a new force called `forceByMass`, and we applied it to the middle sphere.

Test the movie and you will see both the middle and the right spheres jump at the same height:

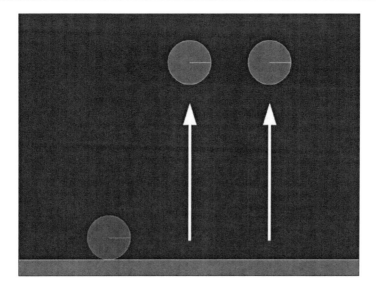

And the output window confirms what we've seen:

- **Sphere 0:410**
- **Sphere 1:80**
- **Sphere 2:80**

Middle and right spheres now react in the same way, while the left sphere still remains in its position.

What's wrong with it? It's a matter of time. While an impulse is applied in a single instant, a force needs to be applied over time, which dealing with physics is normally measured in seconds. This means if we want the left sphere to react like its sisters, we should multiply middle sphere force by the amount of steps required to generate a second of simulation.

Applying a force to get a linear velocity

As the `Step` method works with a time step of 1/30 seconds, we need to multiply the force by 30, so let's change the `Main` function in the following way:

```
public function Main() {
  world=new b2World(new b2Vec2(0,10),true);
  debugDraw();
  floor();
  sphereVector=new Vector.<b2Body>();
  for (var i:int=0; i<3; i++) {
```

Applying Forces to Bodies

```
        sphereVector.push(sphere(170+i*150,410,40));
    }
    var force:b2Vec2=new b2Vec2(0,-15);
    var forceByMass:b2Vec2=force.Copy();
    forceByMass.Multiply(sphereVector[1].GetMass());
    var forceByMassByTime:b2Vec2=forceByMass.Copy();
    forceByMassByTime.Multiply(30);
    var sphereCenter:b2Vec2=sphereVector[0].GetWorldCenter();
    sphereVector[0].ApplyForce(forceByMassByTime,sphereCenter);
    sphereCenter=sphereVector[1].GetWorldCenter();
    sphereVector[1].ApplyImpulse(forceByMass,sphereCenter);
    sphereVector[2].SetLinearVelocity(force);
    addEventListener(Event.ENTER_FRAME,updateWorld);
}
```

The concept is the same we applied earlier wherein we create a new force and apply it to the leftmost sphere. As said, I am multiplying the force used for the middle sphere by 30.

Test the movie and now all spheres will react in the same way:

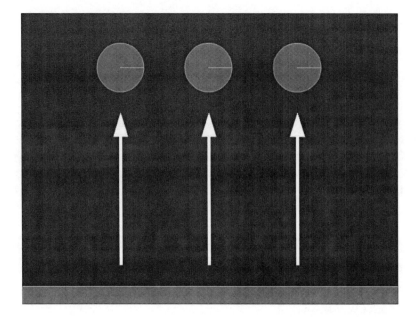

Also the text in the output window confirms that we have managed to move three identical spheres in three different ways:

- **Sphere 0:80**
- **Sphere 1:80**
- **Sphere 2:80**

By now you have learned the basics of forces that you can apply to a body. Anyway, this task was quite easy because you applied forces to sleeping bodies. It would have been much more difficult to achieve the same result with bodies that are already moving or colliding with each other.

While you are free to apply forces in the way you prefer, the following are useful suggestions about which kind of force you should apply according to the game you are developing:

- Set a *linear velocity* when you want to stop a body no matter what it was doing, and apply a brand new motion. In game design, think about a moving platform or an enemy patrolling the area: at each time step you can set its linear velocity and it will move straight in one direction.

- Apply an *impulse* when you want to apply the entire force in one single time step, adding it to existing forces. In game design, a jumping character will use impulses to jump.

- Apply a *force* when you want to give your character a thrust through time, such as a jetpack or the way to control the ball in Ball and Ball Revamped series.

But, above all, experiment! The same things can be done in different ways, it's up to you to find the way to apply forces that fit your needs.

Applying Forces to Bodies

Forces in a real game

Now, let's apply forces to a real world example, Angry Birds.

Angry Birds: Rovio Entertainment Ltd. (www.rovio.com)

This is the first level of the Chrome version, and that's what we are going to build.

At this stage, building an Angry Birds level is not that different from building a Totem Destroyer level. As you can see, I have recycled most of the functions explained in previous chapters. So, the following is how the `Main` class looks now:

```
public class Main extends Sprite {
  private var world:b2World;
  private var worldScale:Number=30;
  public function Main() {
    world=new b2World(new b2Vec2(0,5),true);
    debugDraw();
    floor();
    brick(402,431,140,36);
    brick(544,431,140,36);
    brick(342,396,16,32);
    brick(604,396,16,32);
    brick(416,347,16,130);
    brick(532,347,16,130);
    brick(474,273,132,16);
    brick(474,257,32,16);
```

[64]

```
      brick(445,199,16,130);
      brick(503,199,16,130);
      brick(474,125,58,16);
      brick(474,100,32,32);
      brick(474,67,16,32);
      brick(474,404,64,16);
      brick(450,363,16,64);
      brick(498,363,16,64);
      brick(474,322,64,16);
      addEventListener(Event.ENTER_FRAME,updateWorld);
    }
    private function brick(pX:int,pY:int,w:Number,h:Number):void{
      var bodyDef:b2BodyDef=new b2BodyDef();
      bodyDef.position.Set(pX/worldScale,pY/worldScale);
      bodyDef.type=b2Body.b2_dynamicBody;
      var polygonShape:b2PolygonShape=new b2PolygonShape();
      polygonShape.SetAsBox(w/2/worldScale,h/2/worldScale);
      var fixtureDef:b2FixtureDef=new b2FixtureDef();
      fixtureDef.shape=polygonShape;
      fixtureDef.density=2;
      fixtureDef.restitution=0.4;
      fixtureDef.friction=0.5;
      var theBrick:b2Body=world.CreateBody(bodyDef);
      theBrick.CreateFixture(fixtureDef);
    }
    private function floor():void {
      var bodyDef:b2BodyDef=new b2BodyDef();
      bodyDef.position.Set(320/worldScale,465/worldScale);
      var polygonShape:b2PolygonShape=new b2PolygonShape();
      polygonShape.SetAsBox(320/worldScale,15/worldScale);
      var fixtureDef:b2FixtureDef=new b2FixtureDef();
      fixtureDef.shape=polygonShape;
      fixtureDef.restitution=0.4;
      fixtureDef.friction=0.5;
      var theFloor:b2Body=world.CreateBody(bodyDef);
      theFloor.CreateFixture(fixtureDef);
    }
    private function debugDraw():void {
      var debugDraw:b2DebugDraw=new b2DebugDraw();
      var debugSprite:Sprite=new Sprite();
      addChild(debugSprite);
      debugDraw.SetSprite(debugSprite);
      debugDraw.SetDrawScale(worldScale);
      debugDraw.SetFlags(b2DebugDraw.e_shapeBit);
```

```
      debugDraw.SetFillAlpha(0.5);
      world.SetDebugDraw(debugDraw);
   }
   private function updateWorld(e:Event):void {
      world.Step(1/30,10,10);
      world.ClearForces();
      world.DrawDebugData();
   }
}
```

Really nothing to explain here as it's just copy/paste of old scripts.

Test the movie and you should see your level ready to be destroyed:

Angry Birds: Rovio Entertainment Ltd. (www.rovio.com)

Ok, the pig isn't there, but it does not matter at the moment as you won't be able to kill it until the next chapter. At the moment, let's just destroy its house.

Before we can smash the pigs hideout, we need to draw some graphics representing the sling and the bird. Basically the sling is a circle in which the bird can be moved. The bird itself will be represented at the moment with another circle.

Physics games aren't just a matter of physics

This section has nothing to do with Box2D, and it's just necessary to allow the player to launch the bird. So I am explaining what happens here very quickly, in order to go straight to the point.

Before we start drawing, I want you to know that you can mix physics and non-physics scripts in your game, just like I am doing now. In this case, player interaction is not managed by Box2D, which comes into play once the bird is released.

First, we need some more class-level variables:

```
private var world:b2World;
private var worldScale:Number=30;
private var theBird:Sprite=new Sprite();
private var slingX:int=100;
private var slingY:int=250;
private var slingR:int=75;
```

`theBird` is the sprite representing the draggable bird, `slingX` and `slingY` are the coordinates of the center of the sling in pixels, and `slingR` is the radius of the draggable area of the sling in pixels.

Now, we need to draw some stuff on the stage. We'll draw the big circle representing the sling area, and the small circle representing the bird. Also, we are going to add some listeners to select, draw, and release the bird.

Add the following lines to the `Main` function:

```
public function Main() {
  world=new b2World(new b2Vec2(0,5),true);
  debugDraw();
  floor();
  brick(402,431,140,36);
  brick(544,431,140,36);
  brick(342,396,16,32);
  brick(604,396,16,32);
  brick(416,347,16,130);
  brick(532,347,16,130);
  brick(474,273,132,16);
  brick(474,257,32,16);
  brick(445,199,16,130);
  brick(503,199,16,130);
  brick(474,125,58,16);
```

```
      brick(474,100,32,32);
      brick(474,67,16,32);
      brick(474,404,64,16);
      brick(450,363,16,64);
      brick(498,363,16,64);
      brick(474,322,64,16);
      var slingCanvas:Sprite=new Sprite();
      slingCanvas.graphics.lineStyle(1,0xffffff);
      slingCanvas.graphics.drawCircle(0,0,slingR);
      addChild(slingCanvas);
      slingCanvas.x=slingX;
      slingCanvas.y=slingY;
      theBird.graphics.lineStyle(1,0xffffff);
      theBird.graphics.beginFill(0xffffff);
      theBird.graphics.drawCircle(0,0,15);
      addChild(theBird);
      theBird.x=slingX;
      theBird.y=slingY;
      theBird.addEventListener(MouseEvent.MOUSE_DOWN,birdClick);
      addEventListener(Event.ENTER_FRAME,updateWorld);
   }
```

We are just drawing some stuff, so there's nothing to say. Now, we need a function to be executed when the player presses the mouse on the bird:

```
   private function birdClick(e:MouseEvent):void {
      stage.addEventListener(MouseEvent.MOUSE_MOVE,birdMove);
      stage.addEventListener(MouseEvent.MOUSE_UP,birdRelease);
      theBird.removeEventListener(MouseEvent.MOUSE_DOWN,birdClick);
   }
```

The `birdMove` function will be used as long as the player moves the mouse keeping the mouse button pressed, and will move the bird inside the sling area.

Notice how I am not using Box2D at this stage. There's no need to use it as there's no physics involved when aiming with the bird, and one golden rule is *don't use physics engines when they aren't needed.*

```
   private function birdMove(e:MouseEvent):void {
      theBird.x=mouseX;
      theBird.y=mouseY;
      var distanceX:Number=theBird.x-slingX;
      var distanceY:Number=theBird.y-slingY;
      if (distanceX*distanceX+distanceY*distanceY>slingR*slingR) {
         var birdAngle:Number=Math.atan2(distanceY,distanceX);
```

```
      theBird.x=slingX+slingR*Math.cos(birdAngle);
      theBird.y=slingY+slingR*Math.sin(birdAngle);
   }
}
```

The only thing that really matters in our physics world is the position from which the player releases the bird. According to the bird position and the sling center, we can determine how to fire the bird.

So the `birdRelease` function at the moment will just print the coordinates of the just released bird on the output window.

```
private function birdRelease(e:MouseEvent):void {
   trace("bird released at "+theBird.x+","+theBird.y);
   stage.removeEventListener(MouseEvent.MOUSE_MOVE,birdMove);
   stage.removeEventListener(MouseEvent.MOUSE_UP,birdRelease);
}
```

Test the movie and you will be able to move your bird inside the sling area. Once you release the movie, you will see some text in the output window with the release coordinates.

In the previous screenshot, a bird released at this position will output:

bird released at 44,274

This is all we need to shoot our physics bird.

Applying Forces to Bodies

Placing the physics bird

This is when Box2D comes into play. As we are approximating the bird with a circle, we need to create a Box2D circle in the same point from where the player released the mouse.

Change the `birdRelease` function in the following way:

```
private function birdRelease(e:MouseEvent):void {
    var sphereX:Number=theBird.x/worldScale;
    var sphereY:Number=theBird.y/worldScale;
    var r:Number = 15/worldScale;
    var bodyDef:b2BodyDef=new b2BodyDef();
    bodyDef.position.Set(sphereX,sphereY);
    var circleShape:b2CircleShape=new b2CircleShape(r);
    var fixtureDef:b2FixtureDef=new b2FixtureDef();
    fixtureDef.shape=circleShape;
    fixtureDef.density=4;
    fixtureDef.restitution=0.4;
    fixtureDef.friction=0.5;
    var physicsBird:b2Body=world.CreateBody(bodyDef);
    physicsBird.CreateFixture(fixtureDef);
    removeChild(theBird);
    stage.removeEventListener(MouseEvent.MOUSE_MOVE,birdMove);
    stage.removeEventListener(MouseEvent.MOUSE_UP,birdRelease);
}
```

There's nothing new, we are only creating a static circle with the same size and in the same coordinates of the graphic-only bird.

Test the movie by dragging and releasing the circle. It will turn into a static Box2D circular body.

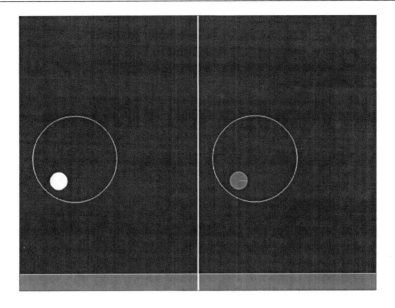

Now we can finally apply the force and make the simulation run.

Shooting the physics bird

We need to add some more lines to the `birdRelease` function:

```
private function birdRelease(e:MouseEvent):void {
   var distanceX:Number=theBird.x-slingX;
   var distanceY:Number=theBird.y-slingY;
   var velocityX:Number=distanceX*-1/5;
   var velocityY:Number=distanceY*-1/5;
   var birdVelocity:b2Vec2=new b2Vec2(velocityX,velocityY);
   var sphereX:Number=theBird.x/worldScale;
   var sphereY:Number=theBird.y/worldScale;
   var r:Number = 15/worldScale;
   var bodyDef:b2BodyDef=new b2BodyDef();
   bodyDef.position.Set(sphereX,sphereY);
   bodyDef.type=b2Body.b2_dynamicBody;
   var circleShape:b2CircleShape=new b2CircleShape(r);
   var fixtureDef:b2FixtureDef=new b2FixtureDef();
   fixtureDef.shape=circleShape;
   fixtureDef.density=4;
   fixtureDef.restitution=0.4;
```

[71]

```
            fixtureDef.friction=0.5;
            var physicsBird:b2Body=world.CreateBody(bodyDef);
            physicsBird.CreateFixture(fixtureDef);
            physicsBird.SetLinearVelocity(birdVelocity);
            removeChild(theBird);
            stage.removeEventListener(MouseEvent.MOUSE_MOVE,birdMove);
            stage.removeEventListener(MouseEvent.MOUSE_UP,birdRelease);
        }
```

Finally, we are adding some forces, so it's time to explain some lines:

```
            var distanceX:Number=theBird.x-slingX;
            var distanceY:Number=theBird.y-slingY;
```

`distanceX` and `distanceY` are two numbers representing the distance between the bird and the center of the sling. The greater the distance, the stronger is the force that will be applied.

```
            var velocityX:Number=distanceX*-1/5;
            var velocityY:Number=distanceY*-1/5;
```

We said the force is related to the distance, so here is how horizontal and vertical velocities are determined. First, we have to multiply them by `-1` because force has to be the opposite of the distance, or the bird will be thrown in the wrong direction. Then we divide the results by 5 just to make it a bit weaker, or we will be firing a supersonic bird.

Changing this value will affect gameplay, so play a bit with it to see what happens.

```
            var birdVelocity:b2Vec2=new b2Vec2(velocityX,velocityY);
```

Finally, velocity variables are used to build the `b2Vec2` object that will assign the force to the bird.

```
            bodyDef.type=b2Body.b2_dynamicBody;
```

Obviously, before we can apply a force to a body, we must set is as dynamic.

```
            physicsBird.SetLinearVelocity(birdVelocity);
```

And now the bird can take off and destroy the pig's nest. I used `SetLinearVelocity` because I want to give different kinds of birds the same velocity if they are released at the same point, no matter their size or mass.

Obviously, I could have used `ApplyForce` or `ApplyImpulse` by multiplying with `birdVelocity` as I had showed at the beginning of the chapter, but why bother? I have my `SetLinearVelocity` method that fits like a glove, and that's it!

Test the movie by dragging and releasing the bird, and you will be able to destroy the scenario.

And as said, here is your Angry Birds level. Still no pigs and camera following the bird, but you'll learn how to do it in the coming chapters.

Summary

In this chapter you learned how to use forces to move bodies in your Box2D world. There's a lot of stuff you can do by applying forces. From a platformer to a pool game, every physics game where the player can move a body in some way implies the use of a force, and now you know how to apply them.

5
Handling Collisions

Given a Box2D world and some moving bodies, sooner or later two of them will collide. Physics games rely on collisions for most gameplay features. When a bird smashes pig's castle in Angry Birds, it is thanks to collisions; when the idol falls down the totem and breaks on the ground, that's due to collisions.

Box2D already does all the required tasks to solve collisions and run the simulation without any coding on our part. By the way, in some situations, we need to interact with collisions for a gameplay purpose.

Think about Angry Birds, hitting hard on a wooden wall will break it, but normal Box2D collision routines do not manage wooden wall breaking. Moreover, if the Totem Destroyer idol hits the ground, the level fails but again Box2D just manages the collisions without caring about the gameplay rules.

That's why sometimes we need to analyze collisions, and luckily Box2D allows us to do it thanks to **contacts**: objects created by Box2D to manage collisions between two fixtures.

In this chapter you will learn how to handle collisions using contacts, and among other things:

- Creating a custom contact listener
- Determining which bodies are colliding
- Determining how hard was a collision
- Looping through all collisions involving a body

By the end of the chapter, you will be able to manage any kind of collision, as well as to complete the Angry Birds and Totem destroyer levels by managing in-game collisions.

Handling Collisions

Checking for collisions

The first step in collision management is to know when two bodies collide and when two bodies do not collide anymore.

Do you remember your very first project, explained in *Chapter 2, Adding Bodies to the World*, with the ball bouncing on the floor?

We'll use it again to get as much information as we can about the collisions between the ball and the floor.

1. Change your `Main` function adding three simple lines, shown as follows:

```
public function Main() {
  world=new b2World(new b2Vec2(0,9.81),true);
  world.SetContactListener(new customContact());
  var bodyDef:b2BodyDef=new b2BodyDef();
  bodyDef.position.Set(320/worldScale,30/worldScale);
  bodyDef.type=b2Body.b2_dynamicBody;
  bodyDef.userData="Ball";
  var circleShape:b2CircleShape;
  circleShape=new b2CircleShape(25/worldScale);
  var fixtureDef:b2FixtureDef=new b2FixtureDef();
  fixtureDef.shape=circleShape;
  fixtureDef.density=1;
  fixtureDef.restitution=0.6;
  fixtureDef.friction=0.1;
  var theBall:b2Body=world.CreateBody(bodyDef);
  theBall.CreateFixture(fixtureDef);
  bodyDef.position.Set(320/worldScale,470/worldScale);
  bodyDef.type=b2Body.b2_staticBody;
  bodyDef.userData="Floor";
  var polygonShape:b2PolygonShape=new b2PolygonShape();
  polygonShape.SetAsBox(320/worldScale,10/worldScale);
  fixtureDef.shape=polygonShape;
  var theFloor:b2Body=world.CreateBody(bodyDef);
  theFloor.CreateFixture(fixtureDef);
  var debugDraw:b2DebugDraw=new b2DebugDraw();
  var debugSprite:Sprite=new Sprite();
  addChild(debugSprite);
  debugDraw.SetSprite(debugSprite);
  debugDraw.SetDrawScale(worldScale);
  debugDraw.SetFlags(b2DebugDraw.e_shapeBit);
  debugDraw.SetFillAlpha(0.5);
  world.SetDebugDraw(debugDraw);
  addEventListener(Event.ENTER_FRAME,updateWorld);
}
```

2. You already know how a `userData` property works, so the core of the function and of the entire chapter lies in the following line:

   ```
   world.SetContactListener(new customContact());
   ```

   Box2D allows us to create a custom contact listener that supports all the events we need to manage collisions, such as when a collision starts and ends, mostly in the same way you are used to dealing with events such as mouse or keyboard events in your AS3 projects.

Box2D built-in collision listener

Without entering too much into the Box2D source code, you should know that it not only solves collisions on its own, but also provides four interesting listeners that allow you to interact with collision, retrieving information, or even modifying some parameters. Everything will be managed within a new class I called `customContact`, thanks to the `SetContactListener` method, which allows us to create custom contact callbacks.

Having said this, create a new file called `customContact.as` and write the following lines of code:

```
package {
  import Box2D.Dynamics.*;
  import Box2D.Collision.*;
  import Box2D.Dynamics.Contacts.*;
  public class customContact extends b2ContactListener {
    override public function BeginContact(contact:b2Contact):void{
      trace("a collision started");
      var fixtureA:b2Fixture=contact.GetFixtureA();
      var fixtureB:b2Fixture=contact.GetFixtureB();
      var bodyA:b2Body=fixtureA.GetBody();
      var bodyB:b2Body=fixtureB.GetBody();
      trace("first body: "+bodyA.GetUserData());
      trace("second body: "+bodyB.GetUserData());
      trace("--------------------------");
    }
    override public function EndContact(contact:b2Contact):void{
      trace("a collision ended");
      var fixtureA:b2Fixture=contact.GetFixtureA();
      var fixtureB:b2Fixture=contact.GetFixtureB();
      var bodyA:b2Body=fixtureA.GetBody();
      var bodyB:b2Body=fixtureB.GetBody();
```

```
        trace("first body: "+bodyA.GetUserData());
        trace("second body: "+bodyB.GetUserData());
        trace("--------------------------");
      }
    }
  }
}
```

The purpose of the `customContact` class is to override Box2D functions called `BeginContact` and `EndContact`, which by default don't do anything, and get some information about the collision.

Trace the beginning and the end of a collision

As the names suggest, the **Begin Contact Event** is called when two fixtures begin to overlap, while the **End Contact Event** is called when two fixtures cease to overlap.

1. Let's analyze the `BeginContact` function line by line:

   ```
   var fixtureA:b2Fixture=contact.GetFixtureA();
   var fixtureB:b2Fixture=contact.GetFixtureB();
   ```

   As you can see, `BeginContact` has a `b2Contact` object passed as an argument. It contains all collision information we are looking for at the moment. `GetFixtureA` and `GetFixtureB` methods return the fixtures involved in the collision. I am saving them in `fixtureA` and `fixtureB` variables.

2. Then, as I am looking for bodies, I need to get the body from a fixture. You should already know about the `GetBody` method:

   ```
   var bodyA:b2Body=fixtureA.GetBody();
   var bodyB:b2Body=fixtureB.GetBody();
   ```

3. Now `bodyA` and `bodyB` are the colliding bodies. Time to print some text in the output window:

   ```
   trace("first body: "+bodyA.GetUserData());
   trace("second body: "+bodyB.GetUserData());
   ```

   I am printing their user data, which can be `Floor` or `Ball`.

   The `EndContact` function has the same code, so there's no need to explain it.

4. Test the movie, and each time the ball bounces on the floor, you should see the following output text:

   a collision started

   first body: Floor

   second body: Ball

   \-

   a collision ended

   first body: Floor

   second body: Ball

   \-

   This is great, because now you know exactly when a collision starts and when a collision ends, as well as the bodies that are colliding.

   But the Box2D contact listener is giving us two more callbacks called `PreSolve` and `PostSolve`.

Detect when you are about to solve a collision and when you have solved it

The **Pre-Solve Event** is called after collision detection, but before collision resolution, so you can interact with a collision before it's solved. The **Post-Solve Event** occurs when a collision has been solved, and allows us to know the impulse of the collision.

1. Add the following two functions to the `customContact` class:

   ```
   override public function PreSolve(contact:b2Contact,
   oldManifold:b2Manifold):void {
     if (contact.GetManifold().m_pointCount>0) {
       trace("a collision has been pre solved");
       var fixtureA:b2Fixture=contact.GetFixtureA();
       var fixtureB:b2Fixture=contact.GetFixtureB();
       var bodyA:b2Body=fixtureA.GetBody();
       var bodyB:b2Body=fixtureB.GetBody();
       trace("first body: "+bodyA.GetUserData());
       trace("second body: "+bodyB.GetUserData());
       trace("---------------------------");
     }
   }
   ```

Handling Collisions

2. The `PreSolve` function at the moment has the same code as `BeginContact` and `EndContact`, but the code is executed only if the following `if` statement is true:

   ```
   if (contact.GetManifold().m_pointCount>0) {
   ```

3. Box2D groups contact points into a manifold structure. The `PreSolve` function is sometimes called even if the contact points aren't there in the manifold, so this time we want it to be executed only if there is at least one contact point.

   ```
   override public function PostSolve(contact:b2Contact,
   impulse:b2ContactImpulse):void {
     trace("a collision has been post solved");
     var fixtureA:b2Fixture=contact.GetFixtureA();
     var fixtureB:b2Fixture=contact.GetFixtureB();
     var bodyA:b2Body=fixtureA.GetBody();
     var bodyB:b2Body=fixtureB.GetBody();
     trace("first body: "+bodyA.GetUserData());
     trace("second body: "+bodyB.GetUserData());
     trace("impulse: "+impulse.normalImpulses[0]);
     trace("---------------------------");
   }
   ```

4. The `PostSolve` function also has the same code as the other functions, with the exception of the following line:

   ```
   trace("impulse: "+impulse.normalImpulses[0]);
   ```

   As you can see, the `PostSolve` function has an impulse passed as an argument. The `normalImpulses` property of a `b2ContactImpulse` object returns a vector with all impulses generated by the collisions. We are looking for the first and only impulse, which in other words represents the strength of the collision.

5. Test the movie again, and every time the ball bounces on the floor, you should see the following output text:

   a collision started

   first body: Floor

   second body: Ball

   \-

   a collision has been pre solved

   first body: Floor

   second body: Ball

----

a collision has been post solved

first body: Floor

second body: Ball

impulse: 57.07226654021458

----

a collision ended

first body: Floor

second body: Ball

----

6. At every bounce, all four functions are called, with a decreasing impulse as the ball bounces lower and lower.

   And that's how contact listeners work, the sequence never changes, and following are its steps, from first to last:

   i. Begin Contact Event is called when the collision has been detected.

   ii. Pre-Solve Event is called before the collision is processed.

   iii. Post-Solve Event is called after the collision has been processed.

   iv. End Contact Event is called when there's no more collision, which may not occur if the bodies keep colliding, such as the ball on the floor when it does not bounce anymore.

With these concepts in mind, let's do something interesting with our Totem Destroyer prototype.

Detecting when the idol falls on the floor in Totem Destroyer

We want the player to fail the level if the idol hits the ground, that is the static body at the bottom. Let's perform the following steps to achieve this:

1. Take the last Totem Destroyer we made in *Chapter 3, Interacting with Bodies*, the one with the text field monitoring idol attributes, and assign a custom data to the floor body changing the `floor` function in the following way:

   ```
   private function floor():void {
     var bodyDef:b2BodyDef=new b2BodyDef();
     bodyDef.position.Set(320/worldScale,465/worldScale);
   ```

Handling Collisions

```
    bodyDef.userData="floor";
    var polygonShape:b2PolygonShape=new b2PolygonShape();
    polygonShape.SetAsBox(320/worldScale,15/worldScale);
    var fixtureDef:b2FixtureDef=new b2FixtureDef();
    fixtureDef.shape=polygonShape;
    fixtureDef.restitution=0.4;
    fixtureDef.friction=0.5;
    var theFloor:b2Body=world.CreateBody(bodyDef);
    theFloor.CreateFixture(fixtureDef);
}
```

Now we have a way to identify the floor.

2. At this time, setting up the entire process with listeners and a custom contact class just to check for a single collision (idol on the ground) would be a waste of CPU power. There are several collisions: bricks against bricks, bricks against floor, and idol against brick, but we just need to check if the idol hits the floor.

3. When you want to handle just a small number of collisions, I would suggest you to do it without creating a custom contact listener class, and manage everything on the fly, looping through collisions in a similar way you already learned to loop through bodies.

4. First, we need to import the required class to handle collisions:

```
import flash.display.Sprite;
import flash.events.Event;
import flash.events.MouseEvent;
import flash.text.TextField;
import flash.text.TextFormat;
import Box2D.Dynamics.*;
import Box2D.Collision.*;
import Box2D.Collision.Shapes.*;
import Box2D.Common.Math.*;
import Box2D.Dynamics.Contacts.*;
```

5. Then, a Boolean variable called `gameOver` will allow us to store the game state. A `true` value means the idol touched the ground and the level failed; a `false` value means the idol is still in the game. Its default value is `false` because at the beginning of the level the idol is alive.

```
private var world:b2World;
private var worldScale:Number=30;
private var textMon:TextField = new TextField();
private var textFormat:TextFormat = new TextFormat();
private var gameOver:Boolean=false;
```

Chapter 5

6. Most of the new code needs to be written in the `updateWorld` function. The idea is to check for idol collisions at every world step rather than setting up listeners.

   Obviously this will be done only if the game is not over yet, so we are changing the `updateWorld` function in the following way:

```
private function updateWorld(e:Event):void {
var radToDeg:Number=180/Math.PI;
world.Step(1/30,10,10);
world.ClearForces();
if (!gameOver) {
  for (var b:b2Body=world.GetBodyList();
   b; b=b.GetNext()) {
    if (b.GetUserData()=="idol") {
      var position:b2Vec2=b.GetPosition();
      var xPos:Number=Math.round(position.x*worldScale);
      textMon.text=xPos.toString();
      textMon.appendText(",");
      var yPos:Number=Math.round(position.y*worldScale);
      textMon.appendText(yPos.toString());
      textMon.appendText("\nangle: ");
      var angle:Number=Math.round(b.GetAngle()*radToDeg);
      textMon.appendText(angle.toString());
      textMon.appendText("\nVelocity: ");
      var velocity:b2Vec2=b.GetLinearVelocity();
      var xVel:Number=Math.round(velocity.x*worldScale);
      textMon.appendText(xVel.toString());
      textMon.appendText(",");
      var yVel:Number=Math.round(velocity.y*worldScale);
      textMon.appendText(yVel.toString());
      for (var c:b2ContactEdge=b.GetContactList();
       c; c=c.next) {
        var contact:b2Contact=c.contact;
        var fixtureA:b2Fixture=contact.GetFixtureA();
        var fixtureB:b2Fixture=contact.GetFixtureB();
        var bodyA:b2Body=fixtureA.GetBody();
        var bodyB:b2Body=fixtureB.GetBody();
        var userDataA:String=bodyA.GetUserData();
        var userDataB:String=bodyB.GetUserData();
        if (userDataA=="floor" && userDataB=="idol") {
          levelFailed();
        }
        if (userDataA=="idol" && userDataB=="floor") {
```

Handling Collisions

```
            levelFailed();
        }
       }
      }
     }
   }
  }
 world.DrawDebugData();
}
```

And the core of the script lies in the following line:

```
for (var c:b2ContactEdge=b.GetContactList(); c; c=c.next) {
```

With the same concept applied to the `GetBodyList` method to scan through all bodies in the Box2D world, `GetContactList` allows us to scan through all contacts of a single body, in this case the idol, as this loop is executed only if we are dealing with the idol.

`b2ContactEdge` is used to connect bodies and contacts together, and as we are looking for the contacts, we must retrieve for each `b2ContactEdge` object the `b2Contact` object, which we are so used to working with now. So we will gain access to the contact in the following way:

```
var contact:b2Contact=c.contact;
```

At this time, the loop is very similar to the callback functions explained at the beginning of the chapter. I also wrote the code in the same way to let you see it's the same concept, although in this case the following code:

```
if (userDataA=="floor" && userDataB=="idol") {
  levelFailed();
}
if (userDataA=="idol" && userDataB=="floor") {
  levelFailed();
}
```

Could also have been written as follows:

```
if (userDataA=="floor" || userDataB=="floor") {
  levelFailed();
}
```

This is because we already know the idol is one of the two bodies involved in the collision.

7. The `levelFailed` function just handles some kind of game over screen, removing the `click` listener so the player cannot destroy bricks anymore, setting the `gameOver` variable to `true` and displaying a game over text.

```
private function levelFailed():void {
  textMon.text="Oh no, poor idol!!!";
  stage.removeEventListener
    (MouseEvent.CLICK,destroyBrick);
  gameOver=true;
}
```

8. Test the game, make the idol fall on the ground, and the game is over:

This was quite easy as there was only one collision to care about. What about the Angry Birds game where there are pigs to kill and bricks to destroy?

Destroying bricks and killing pigs in Angry Birds

Take the last example of *Chapter 4, Applying Forces to Bodies*, the one with the working sling, and let's start working on it.

1. First, as usual, let's add some custom data to bricks, giving them a name in the `brick` function:

```
private function brick(pX:int,pY:int,w:Number,h:Number):void {
  var bodyDef:b2BodyDef=new b2BodyDef();
  bodyDef.position.Set(pX/worldScale,pY/worldScale);
```

Handling Collisions

```
    bodyDef.type=b2Body.b2_dynamicBody;
    bodyDef.userData="brick";
    var polygonShape:b2PolygonShape=new b2PolygonShape();
    polygonShape.SetAsBox(w/2/worldScale,h/2/worldScale);
    var fixtureDef:b2FixtureDef=new b2FixtureDef();
    fixtureDef.shape=polygonShape;
    fixtureDef.density=2;
    fixtureDef.restitution=0.4;
    fixtureDef.friction=0.5;
    var theBrick:b2Body=world.CreateBody(bodyDef);
    theBrick.CreateFixture(fixtureDef);
}
```

2. Then, obviously, let's give the birds something to kill. It's time to create pigs, which are represented as circle shapes. There's nothing new in the `pig` function, which just creates a circle given horizontal and vertical coordinates and a radius, all in pixels.

```
private function pig(pX:int,pY:int,r:Number):void {
    var bodyDef:b2BodyDef=new b2BodyDef();
    bodyDef.position.Set(pX/worldScale,pY/worldScale);
    bodyDef.type=b2Body.b2_dynamicBody;
    bodyDef.userData="pig";   var pigShape:b2CircleShape=
      new b2CircleShape(r/worldScale);
    var fixtureDef:b2FixtureDef=new b2FixtureDef();
    fixtureDef.shape=pigShape;
    fixtureDef.density=1;
    fixtureDef.restitution=0.4;
    fixtureDef.friction=0.5;
    var thePig:b2Body=world.CreateBody(bodyDef);
    thePig.CreateFixture(fixtureDef);
}
```

Also notice pig's custom data.

3. In the `Main` function this time, we need to create a custom contact listener because there are a lot of collisions to manage. Luckily, you already know how to do it. Also, don't forget to create the pig.

```
public function Main() {
    world=new b2World(new b2Vec2(0,5),true);
    world.SetContactListener(new customContact());
    debugDraw();
    floor();
    brick(402,431,140,36);
    brick(544,431,140,36);
```

```
            brick(342,396,16,32);
            brick(604,396,16,32);
            brick(416,347,16,130);
            brick(532,347,16,130);
            brick(474,273,132,16);
            brick(474,257,32,16);
            brick(445,199,16,130);
            brick(503,199,16,130);
            brick(474,125,58,16);
            brick(474,100,32,32);
            brick(474,67,16,32);
            brick(474,404,64,16);
            brick(450,363,16,64);
            brick(498,363,16,64);
            brick(474,322,64,16);
            pig(474,232,16);
            var slingCanvas:Sprite=new Sprite();
            slingCanvas.graphics.lineStyle(1,0xffffff);
            slingCanvas.graphics.drawCircle(0,0,slingR);
            addChild(slingCanvas);
            slingCanvas.x=slingX;
            slingCanvas.y=slingY;
            theBird.graphics.lineStyle(1,0xffffff);
            theBird.graphics.beginFill(0xffffff);
            theBird.graphics.drawCircle(0,0,15);
            addChild(theBird);
            theBird.x=slingX;
            theBird.y=slingY;
            theBird.addEventListener
              (MouseEvent.MOUSE_DOWN,birdClick);
            addEventListener(Event.ENTER_FRAME,updateWorld);
        }
```

4. The core of this project now lies in the `customContact` class, which you will create in the `customContact.as` file:

```
    package {
       import Box2D.Dynamics.*;
       import Box2D.Collision.*;
       import Box2D.Dynamics.Contacts.*;
       public class customContact extends b2ContactListener {
          private const KILLBRICK:Number=25;
          private const KILLPIG:Number=5;
          override public function PostSolve(contact:b2Contact,
            impulse:b2ContactImpulse):void {
```

```
            var fixtureA:b2Fixture=contact.GetFixtureA();
            var fixtureB:b2Fixture=contact.GetFixtureB();
            var dataA:String=fixtureA.GetBody().GetUserData();
            var dataB:String=fixtureB.GetBody().GetUserData();
            var force:Number=impulse.normalImpulses[0];
            switch (dataA) {
              case "pig" :
                if (force>KILLPIG) {
                   fixtureA.GetBody().SetUserData("remove");
                }
                break;
              case "brick" :
                if (force>KILLBRICK) {
                   fixtureA.GetBody().SetUserData("remove");
                }
                break;
            }
            switch (dataB) {
              case "pig" :
                if (force>KILLPIG) {
                   fixtureB.GetBody().SetUserData("remove");
                }
                break;
              case "brick" :
                if (force>KILLBRICK) {
                   fixtureB.GetBody().SetUserData("remove");
                }
                break;
            }
          }
        }
      }
    }
```

5. You have already learned at the beginning of this chapter how things work in the `customContact` class. Anyway, let's take a recap:

```
private const KILLBRICK:Number=25;
private const KILLPIG:Number=5;
```

`KILLBRICK` and `KILLPIG` are two constants with the amount of impulse needed to destroy a brick or kill a pig, respectively.

This means, a brick will be destroyed if involved in a collision that generates an impulse greater than 25 Newton-seconds, while a pig will die if involved in a collision that generates an impulse greater than 5 Newton-seconds.

These are two arbitrary values I have set just to show you how to make things work, and you can change them as you want. Just remember, this will heavily affect gameplay. Setting these values too high will generate indestructible bricks and immortal pigs, while setting them too low can even make the structure collapse due to its weight. It's up to you.

Also, in the original Angry Birds game there are different kinds of materials, such as glass and wood, which affect bricks' impulse needed to be destroyed. You should be able to set materials as you already did during the making of Totem Destroyer. Anyway, don't worry about it as you will fix it later.

6. Time to know which fixtures collided:
   ```
   var fixtureA:b2Fixture=contact.GetFixtureA();
   var fixtureB:b2Fixture=contact.GetFixtureB();
   ```

7. And the custom data of their bodies:
   ```
   var dataA:String=fixtureA.GetBody().GetUserData();
   var dataB:String=fixtureB.GetBody().GetUserData();
   ```

8. Finally, the force of the collision:
   ```
   var force:Number=impulse.normalImpulses[0];
   ```

9. Now we have all the information needed to see what happened during each collision. Time to take some decisions:
   ```
   switch (dataA) {
     case "pig" :
       if (force>KILLPIG) {
         fixtureA.GetBody().SetUserData("remove");
       }
       break;
     case "brick" :
       if (force>KILLBRICK) {
         fixtureA.GetBody().SetUserData("remove");
       }
       break;
   }
   ```

10. Starting from the first body, we check with a `switch` statement if we are dealing with a brick or with a pig, then we see if the collision was hard enough to destroy/kill it.

Handling Collisions

In this case, we won't destroy/kill it at once, but we are going to delegate it to the `updateWorld` function after performing the step. We don't want to remove bodies from the world while the step is currently being calculated, so we just mark it as a body to be removed changing its custom data in the following way:

```
fixtureA.GetBody().SetUserData("remove");
```

11. The same concept is then applied to the second body, and finally in the `updateWorld` function all bodies marked with `remove` will be destroyed.

```
private function updateWorld(e:Event):void {
  world.Step(1/30,10,10);
  world.ClearForces();
  for (var b:b2Body=world.GetBodyList();
   b; b=b.GetNext()) {
    if (b.GetUserData()=="remove") {
      world.DestroyBody(b);
    }
  }
  world.DrawDebugData();
}
```

12. Test the movie, aim and shoot, and you should see bricks and pigs being removed from the world.

That's it, your Angry Birds level is developing more and more as you learn new Box2D features.

Summary

In this chapter, you learned how to interact with collisions both using a custom listener and looping through all collisions of a single body. You also dramatically improved Totem Destroyer and Angry Birds prototypes.

Are you already able to create bricks with different strengths, and display a message when the player kills the bird? You should be!

6
Joints and Motors

All kinds of bodies you've met until now have something in common: they are free and do not depend on each other, unless they collide. Sometimes you may want to constrain bodies to each other. If you think about Crush the Castle game, the siege machine is made by a series of bodies connected together in some way.

Box2D allows us to create constraints between bodies with **joints**. Joints allow us to build complex objects and give more realism to our games.

In this chapter you will learn how to create the most common types of joints, and you will discover, among other things, how to:

- Pick, drag, and drop bodies with mouse joints
- Keep bodies at a given distance with distance joints
- Make bodies rotate using revolute joints
- Give life to your games using motors

By the end of the chapter, you will be able to destroy the Angry Birds level with a siege machine.

Anyway, joints can also be used to interact with bodies, by picking and dragging them with the mouse. This is the first joint you are about to learn.

Picking and dragging bodies – mouse joints

Hard things first; we are going to start with one of the most difficult joints. Sad but necessary, as it will allow us to create and test other joints easily.

Joints and Motors

A **mouse joint** allows a player to move bodies with the mouse, and we will create it with the following features:

- Pick a body by clicking on it
- Move a body following the mouse as long as the button is pressed
- Release a body once the button is released

Some quiet before the storm; the beginning of this process does not differ to other scripts you have already mastered through the book.

1. So, we are importing the required classes:

   ```
   import flash.display.Sprite;
   import flash.events.Event;
   import flash.events.MouseEvent;
   import Box2D.Dynamics.*;
   import Box2D.Collision.*;
   import Box2D.Collision.Shapes.*;
   import Box2D.Common.Math.*;
   ```

2. Then we need the class-level variables for the world itself, and the conversion from pixels to meters:

   ```
   private var world:b2World;
   private var worldScale:Number=30;
   ```

   And even the `Main` function has nothing new, as it just places two box shapes on the stage: the big static ground and a smaller dynamic box on it.

   ```
   public function Main() {
     world=new b2World(new b2Vec2(0,9.81),true);
     debugDraw();
     var bodyDef:b2BodyDef=new b2BodyDef();
     bodyDef.position.Set(320/worldScale,470/worldScale);
     var polygonShape:b2PolygonShape=new b2PolygonShape();
     polygonShape.SetAsBox(320/worldScale,10/worldScale);
     var fixtureDef:b2FixtureDef=new b2FixtureDef();
     fixtureDef.shape=polygonShape;
     var groundBody:b2Body=world.CreateBody(bodyDef);
     groundBody.CreateFixture(fixtureDef);
     bodyDef.position.Set(320/worldScale,430/worldScale);
     bodyDef.type=b2Body.b2_dynamicBody;
     polygonShape.SetAsBox(30/worldScale,30/worldScale);
     fixtureDef.density=1;
     fixtureDef.friction=0.5;
     fixtureDef.restitution=0.2;
   ```

```
    var box2:b2Body=world.CreateBody(bodyDef);
    box2.CreateFixture(fixtureDef);
    addEventListener(Event.ENTER_FRAME,updateWorld);
    stage.addEventListener(MouseEvent.MOUSE_DOWN,
      createJoint);
}
```

3. Don't worry about the `createJoint` callback function in the mouse down listener. At the moment we aren't creating any joint, so we are just querying the world in the same way we did when we learned how to destroy bodies.

```
private function createJoint(e:MouseEvent):void {
    world.QueryPoint(queryCallback,mouseToWorld());
}
```

4. Look at the `mouseToWorld` function now. As we are going to work a lot with mouse coordinates, I created a little function to convert mouse position to a `b2Vec2` object with world coordinates.

```
private function mouseToWorld():b2Vec2 {
    return new b2Vec2(mouseX/worldScale,mouseY/worldScale);
}
```

5. And the `queryCallback` function just checks if the clicked body is a dynamic body with the `GetType` method. You are going to drag bodies, so it's obvious you want to check if a body is dynamic. In this step, let's just write some text in the output window:

```
private function queryCallback(fixture:b2Fixture):Boolean {
    var touchedBody:b2Body=fixture.GetBody();
    if (touchedBody.GetType()==b2Body.b2_dynamicBody) {
      trace("will create joint here");
    }
    return false;
}
```

6. In the end, the debug draw function:

```
private function debugDraw():void {
    var debugDraw:b2DebugDraw=new b2DebugDraw();
    var debugSprite:Sprite=new Sprite();
    addChild(debugSprite);
    debugDraw.SetSprite(debugSprite);
    debugDraw.SetDrawScale(worldScale);
    debugDraw.SetFlags(b2DebugDraw.e_shapeBit);
    debugDraw.SetFillAlpha(0.5);
    world.SetDebugDraw(debugDraw);
}
```

Joints and Motors

7. And the update callback:
   ```
   private function updateWorld(e:Event):void {
     world.Step(1/30,10,10);
     world.ClearForces();
     world.DrawDebugData();
   }
   ```

8. Ok, ready to test the movie finally:

9. Click here and there and nothing will happen until you click on the small dynamic box, which will prompt the following text in the output window:

   will create joint here

   And actually, this is where we are creating the mouse joint.

10. Joints are defined in a separate class we have to include:
    ```
    import flash.display.Sprite;
    import flash.events.Event;
    import flash.events.MouseEvent;
    import Box2D.Dynamics.*;
    import Box2D.Collision.*;
    import Box2D.Collision.Shapes.*;
    import Box2D.Common.Math.*;
    import Box2D.Dynamics.Joints.*;
    ```

11. And we also need to declare a new class-level variable which will store our mouse joint:
    ```
    private var world:b2World;
    private var worldScale:Number=30;
    private var mouseJoint:b2MouseJoint;
    ```

    This is quite intuitive: the `b2MouseJoint` class is what we need to handle mouse joints, so I declared a variable of such type, called `mouseJoint`.

12. And finally, let's create the joint. We need to work on the `queryCallback` function once we know the player is trying to pick a dynamic body.

```
private function queryCallback(fixture:b2Fixture):Boolean {
   var touchedBody:b2Body=fixture.GetBody();
   if (touchedBody.GetType()==b2Body.b2_dynamicBody) {
      var jointDef:b2MouseJointDef=new b2MouseJointDef();
      jointDef.bodyA=world.GetGroundBody();
      jointDef.bodyB=touchedBody;
      jointDef.target=mouseToWorld();
      jointDef.maxForce=1000*touchedBody.GetMass();
      mouseJoint=world.CreateJoint(jointDef) as b2MouseJoint;
      stage.addEventListener(MouseEvent.MOUSE_MOVE,moveJoint);
      stage.addEventListener(MouseEvent.MOUSE_UP,killJoint);
   }
   return false;
}
```

This is some new code, so let's dissect it line by line:

```
var jointDef:b2MouseJointDef=new b2MouseJointDef();
```

We are creating a `b2MouseJointDef` object. In the end, creating joints is not that different from creating bodies. In both cases we have a definition with all tuning parameters, and the body/joint itself. So what we just did is the creation of the joint definition.

Now we need to specify some joint parameters, such as the bodies linked by the joint.

```
jointDef.bodyA=world.GetGroundBody();
jointDef.bodyB=touchedBody;
```

`bodyA` and `bodyB` properties specify the bodies linked by the joint. As we are going to link a body with the mouse, `bodyA` will be the **ground body**. The ground body is not the static box we are using as the floor, but an invisible, untouchable body which represents the world itself. In the real world, the ground body is the air which surrounds us. It's everywhere but we can't see it and we can't touch it.

On the other hand, `bodyB` is the body we just clicked, so we are going to say "the clicked body will be pinned to the world, in a given point". Which point? Mouse pointer coordinates of course, thanks to the target property, which allows us to specify such coordinates as a `b2Vec2` object, and this is where the `mouseToWorld` function comes into play:

```
jointDef.target=mouseToWorld();
```

Now you know that you can drag the mouse around the stage, and you expect the body to follow the mouse pointer. Box2D will handle it for you, however you need to specify the force of the joint. The more powerful the force, the more immediate the body response will be when you move the mouse. Just think about elastic holding the body to your mouse pointer. The more the strength of the elastic, the more precise the movement.

The `maxForce` property allows us to decide the maximum force of the joint. I am setting it quite strong, according to body mass:

```
jointDef.maxForce=1000*touchedBody.GetMass();
```

Now everything has been decided, and we are ready to create the joint based upon the definition we just ended. So let's add the joint to the world with the `CreateJoint` method:

```
mouseJoint=world.CreateJoint(jointDef) as b2MouseJoint;
```

13. At the moment we are done with the joint. Anyway, people will expect the body to move as long as they move the mouse, keeping the button pressed, and release the object once they release the button. So at first we need to add two listeners, to detect when the mouse is moved and when the mouse is released:

```
stage.addEventListener(MouseEvent.MOUSE_MOVE,moveJoint);
stage.addEventListener(MouseEvent.MOUSE_UP,killJoint);
```

14. And now, the callback function `moveJoint` will be called each time the mouse is moved, and it just updates the target of the joint. Do you remember? You had previously set the target with the `target` property of `b2MouseJointDef`, and now you can update the target acting directly on `b2MouseJoint` itself with the `SetTarget` method. Where will the new target be placed? On the new mouse position:

```
private function moveJoint(e:MouseEvent):void {
   mouseJoint.SetTarget(mouseToWorld());
}
```

15. The `killJoint` function is called when the mouse button is released, so we are going to remove the joint with the `DestroyJoint` method in the same way you destroyed bodies with `DestroyBody`. Moreover, the joint variable is set to `null`, and obviously the listeners are removed.

```
private function killJoint(e:MouseEvent):void {
   world.DestroyJoint(mouseJoint);
   mouseJoint=null;
   stage.removeEventListener(MouseEvent.MOUSE_MOVE,
    moveJoint);
```

```
    stage.removeEventListener(MouseEvent.MOUSE_UP,
      killJoint);
}
```

Now you can pick another body. Too bad there's only one dynamic body in this world, but we are going to add a lot of stuff in a matter of seconds.

16. Just one last thing, if you want debug draw to display joints, you need to add them to the SetFlags method in the debugDraw function:

```
private function debugDraw():void {
  var debugDraw:b2DebugDraw=new b2DebugDraw();
  var debugSprite:Sprite=new Sprite();
  addChild(debugSprite);
  debugDraw.SetSprite(debugSprite);
  debugDraw.SetDrawScale(worldScale);
  debugDraw.SetFlags
    (b2DebugDraw.e_shapeBit|b2DebugDraw.e_jointBit);
  debugDraw.SetFillAlpha(0.5);
  world.SetDebugDraw(debugDraw);
}
```

17. Test the movie, pick-and-drag the dynamic box. The joint is represented by debug draw with a cyan line, and the arrow represents mouse movement:

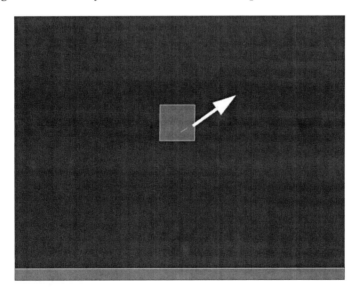

Now that you are able to drag-and-drop bodies, let's create a new box and learn another type of joint.

Keeping bodies at a given distance – distance joints

A **distance joint** is probably the easiest joint to understand and handle. It just sets the distance between two points of two objects, and it will remain constant, no matter what happens.

So we are about to create a new box and link it with the distance joint to the one already in the world. Time to change a bit in our `Main` function:

```
public function Main() {
  world=new b2World(new b2Vec2(0,9.81),true);
  debugDraw();
  var bodyDef:b2BodyDef=new b2BodyDef();
  bodyDef.position.Set(320/worldScale,470/worldScale);
  var polygonShape:b2PolygonShape=new b2PolygonShape();
  polygonShape.SetAsBox(320/worldScale,10/worldScale);
  var fixtureDef:b2FixtureDef=new b2FixtureDef();
  fixtureDef.shape=polygonShape;
  var groundBody:b2Body=world.CreateBody(bodyDef);
  groundBody.CreateFixture(fixtureDef);
  bodyDef.position.Set(320/worldScale,430/worldScale);
  bodyDef.type=b2Body.b2_dynamicBody;
  polygonShape.SetAsBox(30/worldScale,30/worldScale);
  fixtureDef.density=1;
  fixtureDef.friction=0.5;
  fixtureDef.restitution=0.2;
  var box2:b2Body=world.CreateBody(bodyDef);
  box2.CreateFixture(fixtureDef);
  bodyDef.position.Set(420/worldScale,430/worldScale);
  var box3:b2Body=world.CreateBody(bodyDef);
  box3.CreateFixture(fixtureDef);
  var dJoint:b2DistanceJointDef=new b2DistanceJointDef();
  dJoint.bodyA=box2;
  dJoint.bodyB=box3;
  dJoint.localAnchorA=new b2Vec2(0,0);
  dJoint.localAnchorB=new b2Vec2(0,0);
  dJoint.length=100/worldScale;
  var distanceJoint:b2DistanceJoint;
  distanceJoint=world.CreateJoint(dJoint) as b2DistanceJoint;
  addEventListener(Event.ENTER_FRAME,updateWorld);
  stage.addEventListener(MouseEvent.MOUSE_DOWN,createJoint);
}
```

There's no need to comment on the creation of the `box3` body as it's just another box, but I am going to explain the creation of the distance joint line by line.

```
var dJoint:b2DistanceJointDef=new b2DistanceJointDef();
```

You should be used to the Box2D way to create definitions first, so here is `b2DistanceJointDef`, the definition of the distance joint.

Just like the mouse joint, distance joint has its properties to be defined, so we are going to meet `bodyA` and `bodyB` again, this time assigning them the two dynamic boxes:

```
dJoint.bodyA=box2;
dJoint.bodyB=box3;
```

Then we need to define the point in both bodies where the joint has to be pinned. `localAnchorA` and `localAnchorB` properties define the local points where you apply the joints. Pay attention these points are *local*, so if we want to define the joint at the origins of both bodies, their value will be as shown in the following lines of code, irrespective of the position of the bodies:

```
dJoint.localAnchorA=new b2Vec2(0,0);
dJoint.localAnchorB=new b2Vec2(0,0);
```

And finally, the length of the joint, that is the fixed distance between `localAnchorA` and `localAnchorB` points. Boxes have been created at (320,430) and (420,430) respectively, so there's already a distance of 100 pixels. We don't want to change this value, so the `length` property will be:

```
dJoint.length=100/worldScale;
```

Now the joint definition is ready to be created in the world thanks to the `b2DistanceJoint` object—created and added to the world in the old usual way:

```
var distanceJoint:b2DistanceJoint;
distanceJoint=world.CreateJoint(dJoint) as b2DistanceJoint;
```

Joints and Motors

Now you can test the movie. Pick-and-drag each dynamic body, but the distance between body origins won't change, thanks to distance joint.

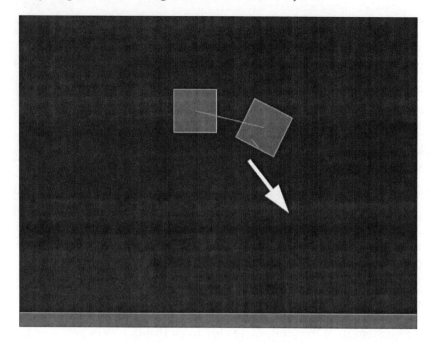

While you can do a lot of stuff with mouse and distance joints, there is another joint which is a life saver in game design: the **revolute joint**.

Making bodies rotate around a point – revolute joints

Revolute joints force two bodies to be pinned in a common anchor point, leaving only a single degree of freedom: the rotation around the anchor point. One of the most common uses of revolute joints is the creation of wheels and cogs.

We will create wheels later when we build the siege machine. At the moment, I just want to add another box to our script and pin it to the ground body to make you see how to interact with revolute joints. We need to make only some changes in the `Main` function:

```
public function Main() {
   world=new b2World(new b2Vec2(0,9.81),true);
   debugDraw();
   var bodyDef:b2BodyDef=new b2BodyDef();
```

```
            bodyDef.position.Set(320/worldScale,470/worldScale);
            var polygonShape:b2PolygonShape=new b2PolygonShape();
            polygonShape.SetAsBox(320/worldScale,10/worldScale);
            var fixtureDef:b2FixtureDef=new b2FixtureDef();
            fixtureDef.shape=polygonShape;
            var groundBody:b2Body=world.CreateBody(bodyDef);
            groundBody.CreateFixture(fixtureDef);
            bodyDef.position.Set(320/worldScale,430/worldScale);
            bodyDef.type=b2Body.b2_dynamicBody;
            polygonShape.SetAsBox(30/worldScale,30/worldScale);
            fixtureDef.density=1;
            fixtureDef.friction=0.5;
            fixtureDef.restitution=0.2;
            var box2:b2Body=world.CreateBody(bodyDef);
            box2.CreateFixture(fixtureDef);
            bodyDef.position.Set(420/worldScale,430/worldScale);
            var box3:b2Body=world.CreateBody(bodyDef);
            box3.CreateFixture(fixtureDef);
            var dJoint:b2DistanceJointDef=new b2DistanceJointDef();
            dJoint.bodyA=box2;
            dJoint.bodyB=box3;
            dJoint.localAnchorA=new b2Vec2(0,0);
            dJoint.localAnchorB=new b2Vec2(0,0);
            dJoint.length=100/worldScale;
            var distanceJoint:b2DistanceJoint;
            distanceJoint=world.CreateJoint(dJoint) as b2DistanceJoint;
            bodyDef.position.Set(320/worldScale,240/worldScale);
            var box4:b2Body=world.CreateBody(bodyDef);
            box4.CreateFixture(fixtureDef);
            var rJoint:b2RevoluteJointDef=new b2RevoluteJointDef();
            rJoint.bodyA=box4;
            rJoint.bodyB=world.GetGroundBody();
            rJoint.localAnchorA=new b2Vec2(0,0);
            rJoint.localAnchorB=box4.GetWorldCenter();
            var revoluteJoint:b2RevoluteJoint;
            revoluteJoint=world.CreateJoint(rJoint) as b2RevoluteJoint;
            addEventListener(Event.ENTER_FRAME,updateWorld);
            stage.addEventListener(MouseEvent.MOUSE_DOWN,createJoint);
        }
```

As usual, there's nothing to say about the creation of the box4 body, and I am going to explain line-by-line joint creation, which starts with the definition of b2RevoluteJointDef:

```
    var rJoint:b2RevoluteJointDef=new b2RevoluteJointDef();
```

Joints and Motors

The process continues in the same way as before, with the assignment of `bodyA` and `bodyB` properties, in this case the last box we created and the ground body:

```
rJoint.bodyA=box4;
rJoint.bodyB=world.GetGroundBody();
```

Now, the local anchor points relative to the bodies, in this case the origin of the box and the same point in world coordinates.

```
rJoint.localAnchorA=new b2Vec2(0,0);
rJoint.localAnchorB=box4.GetWorldCenter();
```

And now, the creation of the revolute joint itself:

```
var revoluteJoint:b2RevoluteJoint;
revoluteJoint=world.CreateJoint(rJoint) as b2RevoluteJoint;
```

Test the movie and interact with the newly created box: try to drag it, place the other boxes over it, do anything you want. There is no way to move it, as it will just rotate around its anchor point.

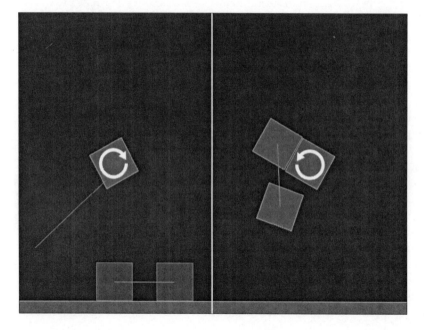

There are more types of joints supported by Box2D, but listing and explaining all joints is beyond the scope of this book. I want you to learn how to make Box2D powered games, and with mouse, distance, and revolute joints you can already do almost everything you want. Refer to the official docs for the complete list of joints http://box2d.org/manual.pdf.

So, rather than making a pointless list of all possible Box2D joints, I will show you something that is strictly related to game development: a siege machine.

When Angry Birds meets Crush the Castle

What if birds had a siege machine? Let's explore this gameplay, but first let me explain which kind of siege machine I want to build using only distance and revolute joints.

The siege machine consists of two carts mounted on wheels. The first cart can be controlled by the player and acts as a truck tractor. The second cart is just a trailer but has something between a trebuchet and a morning star mounted on it.

A bit confused? Let me show you the prototype:

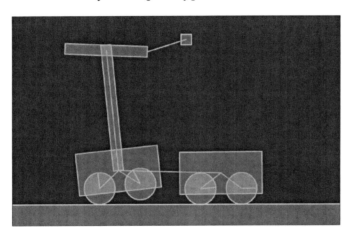

There is a lot to do, so let's start running. What do we need to include in our package?

1. First, the same old classes, `Joints` included:
   ```
   import flash.display.Sprite;
   import flash.events.Event;
   import Box2D.Dynamics.*;
   import Box2D.Collision.*;
   import Box2D.Collision.Shapes.*;
   import Box2D.Common.Math.*;
   import Box2D.Dynamics.Joints.*;
   ```

2. And obviously the class-level variables you are already used to now:
   ```
   private var world:b2World;
   private var worldScale:Number=30;
   ```

Joints and Motors

3. The beginning of this step is not that different from what you have already done a thousand times through this book. The `Main` function is shown as follows:

```
public function Main() {
  world=new b2World(new b2Vec2(0,5),true);
  debugDraw();
  ground();
  var frontCart:b2Body=addCart(200,430);
  var rearCart:b2Body=addCart(100,430);
  addEventListener(Event.ENTER_FRAME,updateWorld);
}
```

4. As usual we create a new world, a debug draw routine, a ground, and a listener is added. Just to be sure to explain everything, the `ground` function, which as usual creates a big static body to be used as a ground, is shown as follows:

```
private function ground():void {
  var bodyDef:b2BodyDef=new b2BodyDef();
  bodyDef.position.Set(320/worldScale,470/worldScale);
  var polygonShape:b2PolygonShape=new b2PolygonShape();
  polygonShape.SetAsBox(320/worldScale,10/worldScale);
  var fixtureDef:b2FixtureDef=new b2FixtureDef();
  fixtureDef.shape=polygonShape;
  var groundBody:b2Body=world.CreateBody(bodyDef);
  groundBody.CreateFixture(fixtureDef);
}
```

5. The only new thing in the `Main` function is the `addCart` function, which just adds a box shape at a given coordinate, so all in all there's nothing new yet:

```
private function addCart(pX:Number,pY:Number):b2Body {
  var bodyDef:b2BodyDef=new b2BodyDef();
  bodyDef.position.Set(pX/worldScale,pY/worldScale);
  var polygonShape:b2PolygonShape=new b2PolygonShape();
  polygonShape.SetAsBox(40/worldScale,20/worldScale);
  var fixtureDef:b2FixtureDef=new b2FixtureDef();
  fixtureDef.shape=polygonShape;
  fixtureDef.density=1;
  fixtureDef.restitution=0.5;
  fixtureDef.friction=0.5;
  var body:b2Body=world.CreateBody(bodyDef);
  body.CreateFixture(fixtureDef);
  var frontWheel:b2Body=addWheel(pX+20,pY+15);
  var rearWheel:b2Body=addWheel(pX-20,pY+15);
  return body;
}
```

6. At the end of the function, before returning the body, there are two calls to the `addWheel` function, which creates a sphere in a given coordinate. Nothing new again, but you'll see how our siege machine will take shape.

   ```
   private function addWheel(pX:Number,pY:Number):b2Body {
     var bodyDef:b2BodyDef=new b2BodyDef();
     bodyDef.position.Set(pX/worldScale,pY/worldScale);
     var circleShape:b2CircleShape=new b2CircleShape(0.5);
     var fixtureDef:b2FixtureDef=new b2FixtureDef();
     fixtureDef.shape=circleShape;
     fixtureDef.density=1;
     fixtureDef.restitution=0.5;
     fixtureDef.friction=0.5;
     var body:b2Body=world.CreateBody(bodyDef);
     body.CreateFixture(fixtureDef);
     return body;
   }
   ```

7. We complete the class with the `debugDraw` function, which also shows joints:

   ```
   private function debugDraw():void {
     var debugDraw:b2DebugDraw=new b2DebugDraw();
     var debugSprite:Sprite=new Sprite();
     addChild(debugSprite);
     debugDraw.SetSprite(debugSprite);
     debugDraw.SetDrawScale(worldScale);
     debugDraw.SetFlags
       (b2DebugDraw.e_shapeBit|b2DebugDraw.e_jointBit);
     debugDraw.SetFillAlpha(0.5);
     world.SetDebugDraw(debugDraw);
   }
   ```

8. And finally the `updateWorld` function:

   ```
   private function updateWorld(e:Event):void {
     world.Step(1/30,10,10);
     world.ClearForces();
     world.DrawDebugData();
   }
   ```

Joints and Motors

9. At this time, two static carts will be created. Test the movie and check if everything seems ok:

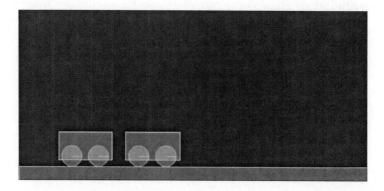

 Remember, when you're building something new with Box2D, always start with static bodies to what your level is going to look, with no gravity, forces, and collisions.

Now that everything looks fine, let's make bodies dynamic and add required joints.

10. Start making wheels and carts dynamic by adding the `type` property in both `addWheel` and `addCart` functions. The `addWheel` function is shown as follows:

```
private function addWheel(pX:Number,pY:Number):b2Body {
  var bodyDef:b2BodyDef=new b2BodyDef();
  bodyDef.position.Set(pX/worldScale,pY/worldScale);
  bodyDef.type=b2Body.b2_dynamicBody;
  var circleShape:b2CircleShape=new b2CircleShape(0.5);
  var fixtureDef:b2FixtureDef=new b2FixtureDef();
  fixtureDef.shape=circleShape;
  fixtureDef.density=1;
  fixtureDef.restitution=0.5;
  fixtureDef.friction=0.5;
  var body:b2Body=world.CreateBody(bodyDef);
  body.CreateFixture(fixtureDef);
  return body;
}
```

11. And the `addCart` function must be modified in the same way:

```
private function addCart(pX:Number,pY:Number):b2Body {
  var bodyDef:b2BodyDef=new b2BodyDef();
  bodyDef.position.Set(pX/worldScale,pY/worldScale);
```

```
    bodyDef.type=b2Body.b2_dynamicBody;
    var polygonShape:b2PolygonShape=new b2PolygonShape();
    polygonShape.SetAsBox(40/worldScale,20/worldScale);
    var fixtureDef:b2FixtureDef=new b2FixtureDef();
    fixtureDef.shape=polygonShape;
    fixtureDef.density=1;
    fixtureDef.restitution=0.5;
    fixtureDef.friction=0.5;
    var body:b2Body=world.CreateBody(bodyDef);
    body.CreateFixture(fixtureDef);
    var frontWheel:b2Body=addWheel(pX+20,pY+15);
    var rearWheel:b2Body=addWheel(pX-20,pY+15);
    var rJoint:b2RevoluteJointDef=new b2RevoluteJointDef();
    rJoint.bodyA=body;
    rJoint.bodyB=frontWheel;
    rJoint.localAnchorA.Set(20/worldScale,15/worldScale);
    rJoint.localAnchorB.Set(0,0);
    var revoluteJoint:b2RevoluteJoint;
    revoluteJoint=world.CreateJoint(rJoint) as b2RevoluteJoint;
    rJoint.bodyB=rearWheel;
    rJoint.localAnchorA.Set(-20/worldScale,15/worldScale);
    revoluteJoint=world.CreateJoint(rJoint) as b2RevoluteJoint;
    return body;
}
```

But it's not over with the code to add in the `addCart` function. As you can see, I added two revolute joints pinning the origin of the each wheel to the cart. Don't worry about collisions as bodies pinned with a revolute joint do not collide.

12. Finally we need a distance joint to manage the truck-trailer thing, to be added in the `Main` function:

```
public function Main() {
    world=new b2World(new b2Vec2(0,5),true);
    debugDraw();
    ground();
    var frontCart:b2Body=addCart(200,430);
    var rearCart:b2Body=addCart(100,430);
    var dJoint:b2DistanceJointDef=new b2DistanceJointDef();
    dJoint.bodyA=frontCart;
    dJoint.bodyB=rearCart;
    dJoint.localAnchorA=new b2Vec2(0,0);
```

```
            dJoint.localAnchorB=new b2Vec2(0,0);
            dJoint.length=100/worldScale;
            var distanceJoint:b2DistanceJoint;
            distanceJoint=world.CreateJoint(dJoint) as b2DistanceJoint;
            addEventListener(Event.ENTER_FRAME,updateWorld);
        }
```

13. And there's nothing new at the moment, but you were able to start building your siege machine anyway. Test the movie:

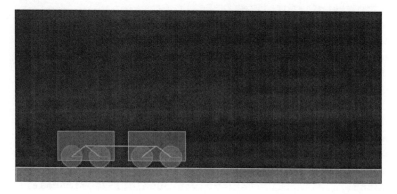

Your carts now have wheels and are linked by a distance joint. Now we must introduce something new to allow players to move the truck.

Controlling joints with motors

Some joints, such as the revolute joint feature motors, which in this case can be used to rotate the joint at a given speed unless a given maximum torque is exceeded.

Learning motors will allow you to develop every kind of car/truck game you see on the Web.

1. To create the truck, we need to apply a motor on the rightmost cart, so in the `addCart` function we are adding an argument to tell us whether it should have a motor or not. Change the `Main` function to specify that `frontCart` will have a motor while `rearCart` won't:

```
public function Main() {
    world=new b2World(new b2Vec2(0,5),true);
    debugDraw();
    ground();
    var frontCart:b2Body=addCart(200,430,true);
    var rearCart:b2Body=addCart(100,430,false);
```

```
            var dJoint:b2DistanceJointDef=new b2DistanceJointDef();
            dJoint.bodyA=frontCart;
            dJoint.bodyB=rearCart;
            dJoint.localAnchorA=new b2Vec2(0,0);
            dJoint.localAnchorB=new b2Vec2(0,0);
            dJoint.length=100/worldScale;
            var distanceJoint:b2DistanceJoint;
            distanceJoint=world.CreateJoint(dJoint) as
             b2DistanceJoint;
            addEventListener(Event.ENTER_FRAME,updateWorld);
        }
```

2. Consequently, the `addCart` function declaration changes too, but this is not interesting. What I would like you to notice are the lines added if `motor` is `true`:

```
        private function
        addCart(pX:Number,pY:Number,motor:Boolean):b2Body {
            var bodyDef:b2BodyDef=new b2BodyDef();
            bodyDef.position.Set(pX/worldScale,pY/worldScale);
            bodyDef.type=b2Body.b2_dynamicBody;
            var polygonShape:b2PolygonShape=new b2PolygonShape();
            polygonShape.SetAsBox(40/worldScale,20/worldScale);
            var fixtureDef:b2FixtureDef=new b2FixtureDef();
            fixtureDef.shape=polygonShape;
            fixtureDef.density=1;
            fixtureDef.restitution=0.5;
            fixtureDef.friction=0.5;
            var body:b2Body=world.CreateBody(bodyDef);
            body.CreateFixture(fixtureDef);
            var frontWheel:b2Body=addWheel(pX+20,pY+15);
            var rearWheel:b2Body=addWheel(pX-20,pY+15);
            var rJoint:b2RevoluteJointDef=new b2RevoluteJointDef();
            rJoint.bodyA=body;
            rJoint.bodyB=frontWheel;
            rJoint.localAnchorA.Set(20/worldScale,15/worldScale);
            rJoint.localAnchorB.Set(0,0);
            if (motor) {
              rJoint.enableMotor=true;
              rJoint.maxMotorTorque=1000;
              rJoint.motorSpeed=5;
            }
            var revoluteJoint:b2RevoluteJoint;
            revoluteJoint=world.CreateJoint(rJoint) as
             b2RevoluteJoint;
            rJoint.bodyB=rearWheel;
```

Joints and Motors

```
    rJoint.localAnchorA.Set(-20/worldScale,15/worldScale);
    revoluteJoint=world.CreateJoint(rJoint) as
     b2RevoluteJoint;
    return body;
}
```

Let's look at the new lines:

`rJoint.enableMotor=true;`

`enableMotor` is a Boolean property of `b2RevoluteJointDef`, the joint definition, and it's a flag to enable joint motor. Its default value is `false`, but setting it to `true` will allow us to add a motor to the revolute joint.

`rJoint.maxMotorTorque=1000;`

The `maxMotorTorque` property defines the maximum torque the motor can apply. The higher the value, the more powerful the motor. Please notice `maxMotorTorque` does not control motor speed, but the maximum torque applicable to reach the desired speed. It's measured in newton meter or N m.

Finally, the `motorSpeed` property sets the desired motor speed, in radians per second:

`rJoint.motorSpeed=5;`

3. In the end, the three motor related lines mean: enable the motor and set its speed to `5` radians per second, using a maximum torque of `1000` N m.
4. Test the movie, and look at your truck running to the right.

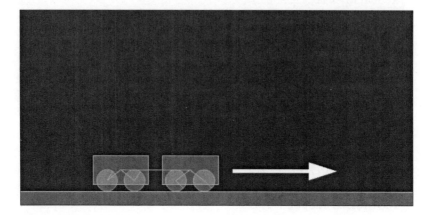

Now you can make the truck move. What about moving the truck with a keyboard input?

Controlling motors with keyboard

We want the player to control the truck with arrow keys. Left arrow key will move the truck to the left and right arrow key will move the truck to the right.

1. To let the player control motors with keyboard, you first need to include the `KeyboardEvent` class, which will allow us to create keyboard listeners:

    ```
    import flash.display.Sprite;
    import flash.events.Event;
    import flash.events.KeyboardEvent;
    import Box2D.Dynamics.*;
    import Box2D.Collision.*;
    import Box2D.Collision.Shapes.*;
    import Box2D.Common.Math.*;
    import Box2D.Dynamics.Joints.*;
    ```

2. Then, we need some new class-level variables:

    ```
    private var world:b2World;
    private var worldScale:Number=30;
    private var left:Boolean=false;
    private var right:Boolean=false;
    private var frj:b2RevoluteJoint;
    private var rrj:b2RevoluteJoint;
    private var motorSpeed:Number=0;
    ```

    `left` and `right` are Boolean variables, which will let us know if left or right arrow keys are being pressed.

    `frj` and `rrj` are the front and rear revolute joint respectively. Variable names are a bit confusing, but I had to use as few characters as I could to give them names for a layout purpose.

    `motorSpeed` is the current motor speed, initially set at zero.

3. In the `Main` function now we add the listeners to trigger when the player presses and releases a key:

    ```
    public function Main() {
        world=new b2World(new b2Vec2(0,5),true);
        debugDraw();
        ground();
        var frontCart:b2Body=addCart(200,430,true);
        var rearCart:b2Body=addCart(100,430,false);
        var dJoint:b2DistanceJointDef=new b2DistanceJointDef();
        dJoint.bodyA=frontCart;
        dJoint.bodyB=rearCart;
        dJoint.localAnchorA=new b2Vec2(0,0);
    ```

Joints and Motors

```
      dJoint.localAnchorB=new b2Vec2(0,0);
      dJoint.length=100/worldScale;
      var distanceJoint:b2DistanceJoint;
      distanceJoint=world.CreateJoint(dJoint) as
       b2DistanceJoint;
      addEventListener(Event.ENTER_FRAME,updateWorld);
      stage.addEventListener(KeyboardEvent.KEY_DOWN,keyPressed);
      stage.addEventListener(KeyboardEvent.KEY_UP,keyReleased);
   }
```

4. And following are the callback functions. When the player presses left or right arrow keys, `left` or `right` become `true`:

```
private function keyPressed(e:KeyboardEvent):void {
   switch (e.keyCode) {
      case 37 :
         left=true;
         break;
      case 39 :
         right=true;
         break;
   }
}
```

In the same way, when the player releases left or right arrow keys, `left` or `right` become `false`:

```
private function keyReleased(e:KeyboardEvent):void {
   switch (e.keyCode) {
      case 37 :
         left=false;
         break;
      case 39 :
         right=false;
         break;
   }
}
```

5. In the `addCart` function there are some changes, but mostly to distinguish revolute joints with motors, which can be controlled with keyboard input and passive revolute joints.

```
private function addCart(pX:Number,pY:Number,motor:Boolean):b2Body
{
   var bodyDef:b2BodyDef=new b2BodyDef();
   bodyDef.position.Set(pX/worldScale,pY/worldScale);
   bodyDef.type=b2Body.b2_dynamicBody;
```

```
var polygonShape:b2PolygonShape=new b2PolygonShape();
polygonShape.SetAsBox(40/worldScale,20/worldScale);
var fixtureDef:b2FixtureDef=new b2FixtureDef();
fixtureDef.shape=polygonShape;
fixtureDef.density=1;
fixtureDef.restitution=0.5;
fixtureDef.friction=0.5;
var body:b2Body=world.CreateBody(bodyDef);
body.CreateFixture(fixtureDef);
var frontWheel:b2Body=addWheel(pX+20,pY+15);
var rearWheel:b2Body=addWheel(pX-20,pY+15);
var rJoint:b2RevoluteJointDef=new b2RevoluteJointDef();
rJoint.bodyA=body;
rJoint.bodyB=frontWheel;
rJoint.localAnchorA.Set(20/worldScale,15/worldScale);
rJoint.localAnchorB.Set(0,0);
if (motor) {
  rJoint.enableMotor=true;
  rJoint.maxMotorTorque=1000;
  rJoint.motorSpeed=0;
  frj=world.CreateJoint(rJoint) as b2RevoluteJoint;
}
else {
  var rj:b2RevoluteJoint;
  rj=world.CreateJoint(rJoint) as b2RevoluteJoint;
}

rJoint.bodyB=rearWheel;
rJoint.localAnchorA.Set(-20/worldScale,15/worldScale);
if (motor) {
  rrj=world.CreateJoint(rJoint) as b2RevoluteJoint;
}
else {
  rj=world.CreateJoint(rJoint) as b2RevoluteJoint;
}
return body;
}
```

Basically, the only differences reside in the variable used to create the revolute joint. Front cart with motor will use `frj` and `rrj` class-level variables to represent revolute joints, while rear car without motors just uses local variables.

Joints and Motors

6. The core of the script is written in the `updateWorld` function, which adjusts the `motorSpeed` variable according to the key being pressed (I also simulate some kind of inertia and friction multiplying it by `0.99` each time), limits the maximum motor speed to `5` or `-5`, and updates the motor speed of the revolute joints.

```
private function updateWorld(e:Event):void {
  if (left) {
    motorSpeed-=0.1;
  }
  if (right) {
    motorSpeed+=0.1;
  }
  motorSpeed*0.99;
  if (motorSpeed>5) {
    motorSpeed=5;
  }
  if (motorSpeed<-5) {
    motorSpeed=-5;
  }
  frj.SetMotorSpeed(motorSpeed);
  rrj.SetMotorSpeed(motorSpeed);
  world.Step(1/30,10,10);
  world.ClearForces();
  world.DrawDebugData();
}
```

7. The `SetMotorSpeed` method directly applied on the revolute joint (not on its definition) allows us to update motor speed on the fly.

8. Test the movie and you will be able to control the truck with left and right arrow keys.

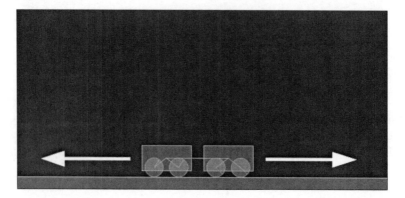

Now we have a working truck with trailer, but don't forget we aren't here to build trucks, but siege machines to destroy pigs' hideouts.

Don't let some bodies collide – filtering collisions

Don't be fooled by the heading: we are going to build the siege machine, it's just that it does not introduce anything new, and I want you to learn something new at every step. The main purpose of this section is to learn collision filtering.

1. First things first, let's build the siege machine. The morning star projectile will be bound to the trailer with a distance joint that we need to be able to destroy to fire the projectile, so we need it as a class level variable:

   ```
   private var world:b2World;
   private var worldScale:Number=30;
   private var left:Boolean=false;
   private var right:Boolean=false;
   private var frj:b2RevoluteJoint;
   private var rrj:b2RevoluteJoint;
   private var motorSpeed:Number=0;
   private var sling:b2DistanceJoint;
   ```

2. The construction of the siege machine itself over the trailer is not complex, there's only a lot of code to write when the `motor` is `false`, that is when we aren't working on the truck.

   ```
   private function addCart(pX:Number,pY:Number,motor:Boolean):b2Body
   {
     var bodyDef:b2BodyDef=new b2BodyDef();
     bodyDef.position.Set(pX/worldScale,pY/worldScale);
     bodyDef.type=b2Body.b2_dynamicBody;
     var polygonShape:b2PolygonShape=new b2PolygonShape();
     polygonShape.SetAsBox(40/worldScale,20/worldScale);
     var fixtureDef:b2FixtureDef=new b2FixtureDef();
     fixtureDef.shape=polygonShape;
     fixtureDef.density=1;
     fixtureDef.restitution=0.5;
     fixtureDef.friction=0.5;
     var body:b2Body=world.CreateBody(bodyDef);
     body.CreateFixture(fixtureDef);
     if (! motor) {
       var armOrigin:b2Vec2=new b2Vec2(0,-60/worldScale);
       var armW:Number=5/worldScale
       var armH:Number=60/worldScale
   ```

Joints and Motors

```
        polygonShape.SetAsOrientedBox(armW,armH,armOrigin);
        body.CreateFixture(fixtureDef);
        bodyDef.position.Set(pX/worldScale,(pY-115)/worldScale);
        polygonShape.SetAsBox(40/worldScale,5/worldScale);
        fixtureDef.shape=polygonShape;
        fixtureDef.filter.categoryBits=0x0002;
        fixtureDef.filter.maskBits=0x0002;
        var arm:b2Body=world.CreateBody(bodyDef);
        arm.CreateFixture(fixtureDef);
        var armJoint:b2RevoluteJointDef;
        armJoint=new b2RevoluteJointDef();
        armJoint.bodyA=body;
        armJoint.bodyB=arm;
        armJoint.localAnchorA.Set(0,-115/worldScale);
        armJoint.localAnchorB.Set(0,0);
        armJoint.enableMotor=true;
        armJoint.maxMotorTorque=1000;
        armJoint.motorSpeed=6;
        var siege:b2RevoluteJoint;
        siege=world.CreateJoint(armJoint) as b2RevoluteJoint;
        var projectileX:Number=(pX-80)/worldScale;
        var projectileY:Number=(pY-115)/worldScale;
        bodyDef.position.Set(projectileX,projectileY);
        polygonShape.SetAsBox(5/worldScale,5/worldScale);
        fixtureDef.shape=polygonShape;
        fixtureDef.filter.categoryBits=0x0004;
        fixtureDef.filter.maskBits=0x0004;
        var projectile:b2Body=world.CreateBody(bodyDef);
        projectile.CreateFixture(fixtureDef);
        var slingJoint:b2DistanceJointDef;
        slingJoint=new b2DistanceJointDef();
        slingJoint.bodyA=arm;
        slingJoint.bodyB=projectile;
        slingJoint.localAnchorA.Set(-40/worldScale,0);
        slingJoint.localAnchorB.Set(0,0);
        slingJoint.length=40/worldScale;
        sling=world.CreateJoint(slingJoint) as b2DistanceJoint;
    }
    var frontWheel:b2Body=addWheel(pX+20,pY+15);
    var rearWheel:b2Body=addWheel(pX-20,pY+15);
    var rJoint:b2RevoluteJointDef=new b2RevoluteJointDef();
    rJoint.bodyA=body;
    rJoint.bodyB=frontWheel;
```

```
        rJoint.localAnchorA.Set(20/worldScale,15/worldScale);
        rJoint.localAnchorB.Set(0,0);
        if (motor) {
          rJoint.enableMotor=true;
          rJoint.maxMotorTorque=1000;
          rJoint.motorSpeed=0;
          frj=world.CreateJoint(rJoint) as b2RevoluteJoint;
        }
        else {
          var rj:b2RevoluteJoint;
          rj=world.CreateJoint(rJoint) as b2RevoluteJoint;
        }
        rJoint.bodyB=rearWheel;
        rJoint.localAnchorA.Set(-20/worldScale,15/worldScale);
        if (motor) {
          rrj=world.CreateJoint(rJoint) as b2RevoluteJoint;
        }
        else {
          rj=world.CreateJoint(rJoint) as b2RevoluteJoint;
        }
        return body;
      }
```

Let's dissect it chunk by chunk:

```
var armOrigin:b2Vec2=new b2Vec2(0,-60/worldScale);
var armW:Number=5/worldScale
var armH:Number=60/worldScale
polygonShape.SetAsOrientedBox(armW,armH,armOrigin);
body.CreateFixture(fixtureDef);
```

These five lines create the vertical bar which goes from the trailer to the morning star. The vertical bar is part of the trailer itself as its fixture has been added to the same body. It's a compound object.

```
bodyDef.position.Set(pX/worldScale,(pY-115)/worldScale);
polygonShape.SetAsBox(40/worldScale,5/worldScale);
fixtureDef.shape=polygonShape;
fixtureDef.filter.categoryBits=0x0002;
fixtureDef.filter.maskBits=0x0002;
var arm:b2Body=world.CreateBody(bodyDef);
arm.CreateFixture(fixtureDef);
```

Joints and Motors

This is the rotating arm, part of the morning star. It has been created as a standalone body as it will be pinned to the trailer's vertical arm with a revolute joint.

```
var armJoint:b2RevoluteJointDef;
armJoint=new b2RevoluteJointDef();
armJoint.bodyA=body;
armJoint.bodyB=arm;
armJoint.localAnchorA.Set(0,-115/worldScale);
armJoint.localAnchorB.Set(0,0);
armJoint.enableMotor=true;
armJoint.maxMotorTorque=1000;
armJoint.motorSpeed=6;
var siege:b2RevoluteJoint;
siege=world.CreateJoint(armJoint) as b2RevoluteJoint;
```

And here is the revolute joint itself. It has a motor to allow the morning star to rotate.

```
var projectileX:Number=(pX-80)/worldScale;
var projectileY:Number=(pY-115)/worldScale;
bodyDef.position.Set(projectileX,projectileY);
polygonShape.SetAsBox(5/worldScale,5/worldScale);
fixtureDef.shape=polygonShape;
fixtureDef.filter.categoryBits=0x0004;
fixtureDef.filter.maskBits=0x0004;
var projectile:b2Body=world.CreateBody(bodyDef);
projectile.CreateFixture(fixtureDef);
```

The projectile—the body which will be launched by the siege machine, the head of the morning star—will be bound to the arm body with a distance joint.

```
slingJoint=new b2DistanceJointDef();
slingJoint.bodyA=arm;
slingJoint.bodyB=projectile;
slingJoint.localAnchorA.Set(-40/worldScale,0);
slingJoint.localAnchorB.Set(0,0);
slingJoint.length=40/worldScale;
sling=world.CreateJoint(slingJoint) as b2DistanceJoint;
```

And finally the distance joint that completes the morning star. Everything seems easy but you shouldn't have missed the following two lines in the creation of the vertical arm:

```
fixtureDef.filter.categoryBits=0x0002;
fixtureDef.filter.maskBits=0x0002;
```

And the following two too during the creation of the projectile:

```
fixtureDef.filter.categoryBits=0x0004;
fixtureDef.filter.maskBits=0x0004;
```

You already know that bodies pinned with a revolute joint do not collide. Unfortunately the projectile is not a part of the revolute joint and will collide with the vertical arm, so the morning star would not work, unless we find a way to prevent vertical arm and projectile collision.

Box2D features **collision filtering**, which allows you to prevent collision among fixtures. Collision filtering allows us to put fixtures in categories with the `categoryBits` property. This way, more fixtures can be placed in one big group. Then, you need to specify for every group which groups they are allowed to collide with, using masking bits.

In the last four lines of code we just saw, the trailer and the projectile are placed into different categories whose masking bits only allow collisions among fixtures inside the same category, so the projectile and the vertical arm will never collide, allowing the morning star to rotate freely. This way, the projectile won't even collide with the ground, but we'll fix it in a minute.

3. One last thing, the player will be able to fire the projectile by destroying the distance joint once the up arrow key is pressed, so we are adding another case in the `switch` statement in the `keyPressed` function:

```
private function keyPressed(e:KeyboardEvent):void {
   switch (e.keyCode) {
     case 37 :
       left=true;
       break;
     case 39 :
       right=true;
       break;
     case 38 :
       world.DestroyJoint(sling);
       break;
   }
}
```

The `DestroyJoint` method removes a joint from the world.

Joints and Motors

4. Test the movie, move the siege machine left and right, and fire with the up arrow key.

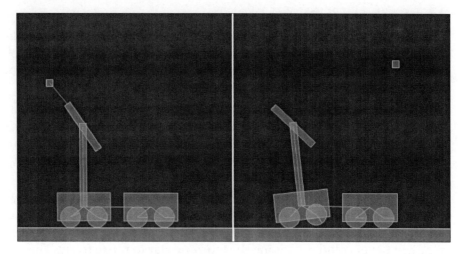

This has been a huge achievement. Building a siege machine with Box2D is not easy, but you managed to do it. It's time to kill some pigs.

Putting it all together

Time to take all of our Box2D knowledge and put it all together, to create the ultimate mix between Angry Birds and Crush the Castle.

1. First, we modify a little the `ground` function to let it create the ground in the same place as we created it during our latest Angry Birds prototype:

```
private function ground():void {
    var bodyDef:b2BodyDef=new b2BodyDef();
    bodyDef.position.Set(320/worldScale,465/worldScale);
    var polygonShape:b2PolygonShape=new b2PolygonShape();
    polygonShape.SetAsBox(320/worldScale,10/worldScale);
    var fixtureDef:b2FixtureDef=new b2FixtureDef();
    fixtureDef.shape=polygonShape;
    var groundBody:b2Body=world.CreateBody(bodyDef);
    groundBody.CreateFixture(fixtureDef);
}
```

Chapter 6

2. Then, we need to update the `Main` function to include the custom listener, the bricks, and the pigs.

```
public function Main() {
    world=new b2World(new b2Vec2(0,5),true);
    world.SetContactListener(new customContact());
    debugDraw();
    ground();
    brick(402,431,140,36);
    brick(544,431,140,36);
    brick(342,396,16,32);
    brick(604,396,16,32);
    brick(416,347,16,130);
    brick(532,347,16,130);
    brick(474,273,132,16);
    brick(474,257,32,16);
    brick(445,199,16,130);
    brick(503,199,16,130);
    brick(474,125,58,16);
    brick(474,100,32,32);
    brick(474,67,16,32);
    brick(474,404,64,16);
    brick(450,363,16,64);
    brick(498,363,16,64);
    brick(474,322,64,16);
    pig(474,232,16);
    var frontCart:b2Body=addCart(200,430,true);
    var rearCart:b2Body=addCart(100,430,false);
    var dJoint:b2DistanceJointDef=new b2DistanceJointDef();
    dJoint.bodyA=frontCart;
    dJoint.bodyB=rearCart;
    dJoint.localAnchorA=new b2Vec2(0,0);
    dJoint.localAnchorB=new b2Vec2(0,0);
    dJoint.length=100/worldScale;
    var distanceJoint:b2DistanceJoint;
    distanceJoint=world.CreateJoint(dJoint) as
        b2DistanceJoint;
    addEventListener(Event.ENTER_FRAME,updateWorld);
    stage.addEventListener(KeyboardEvent.KEY_DOWN,
        keyPressed);
    stage.addEventListener(KeyboardEvent.KEY_UP,keyReleased);
}
```

Joints and Motors

3. Obviously, you must also add `brick` and `pig` functions from the latest Angry Birds prototype, as well as the `customContact` class to handle collisions.
4. Then we modify a bit the `addCart` function, giving a name to our cart parts using custom data, making them heavier—heavy enough to damage the pigs' castle with a small projectile, and we also remove the filtering.

```
private function addCart(pX:Number,pY:Number,motor:Boolean):b2Body
{
  var bodyDef:b2BodyDef=new b2BodyDef();
  bodyDef.position.Set(pX/worldScale,pY/worldScale);
  bodyDef.type=b2Body.b2_dynamicBody;
  bodyDef.userData="cart";
  var polygonShape:b2PolygonShape=new b2PolygonShape();
  polygonShape.SetAsBox(40/worldScale,20/worldScale);
  var fixtureDef:b2FixtureDef=new b2FixtureDef();
  fixtureDef.shape=polygonShape;
  fixtureDef.density=10;
  fixtureDef.restitution=0.5;
  fixtureDef.friction=0.5;
  var body:b2Body=world.CreateBody(bodyDef);
  body.CreateFixture(fixtureDef);
  if (! motor) {
    var armOrigin:b2Vec2=new b2Vec2(0,-60/worldScale);
    var armW:Number=5/worldScale;
    var armH:Number=60/worldScale;
    polygonShape.SetAsOrientedBox(armW,armH,armOrigin);
    body.CreateFixture(fixtureDef);
    bodyDef.position.Set(pX/worldScale,
      (pY-115)/worldScale);
    polygonShape.SetAsBox(40/worldScale,5/worldScale);
    fixtureDef.shape=polygonShape;
    var arm:b2Body=world.CreateBody(bodyDef);
    arm.CreateFixture(fixtureDef);
    var armJoint:b2RevoluteJointDef;
    armJoint=new b2RevoluteJointDef();
    armJoint.bodyA=body;
    armJoint.bodyB=arm;
    armJoint.localAnchorA.Set(0,-115/worldScale);
    armJoint.localAnchorB.Set(0,0);
    armJoint.enableMotor=true;
    armJoint.maxMotorTorque=1000;
    armJoint.motorSpeed=6;
    var siege:b2RevoluteJoint;
    siege=world.CreateJoint(armJoint) as b2RevoluteJoint;
```

```
            var projectileX:Number=(pX-80)/worldScale;
            var projectileY:Number=(pY-115)/worldScale;
            bodyDef.position.Set(projectileX,projectileY);
            bodyDef.userData="projectile";
            polygonShape.SetAsBox(5/worldScale,5/worldScale);
            fixtureDef.shape=polygonShape;
            var projectile:b2Body=world.CreateBody(bodyDef);
            projectile.CreateFixture(fixtureDef);
            var slingJoint:b2DistanceJointDef;
            slingJoint=new b2DistanceJointDef();
            slingJoint.bodyA=arm;
            slingJoint.bodyB=projectile;
            slingJoint.localAnchorA.Set(-40/worldScale,0);
            slingJoint.localAnchorB.Set(0,0);
            slingJoint.length=40/worldScale;
            sling=world.CreateJoint(slingJoint) as b2DistanceJoint;
        }
        var frontWheel:b2Body=addWheel(pX+20,pY+15);
        var rearWheel:b2Body=addWheel(pX-20,pY+15);
        var rJoint:b2RevoluteJointDef=new b2RevoluteJointDef();
        rJoint.bodyA=body;
        rJoint.bodyB=frontWheel;
        rJoint.localAnchorA.Set(20/worldScale,15/worldScale);
        rJoint.localAnchorB.Set(0,0);
        if (motor) {
          rJoint.enableMotor=true;
          rJoint.maxMotorTorque=1000;
          rJoint.motorSpeed=0;
          frj=world.CreateJoint(rJoint) as b2RevoluteJoint;
        }
        else {
          var rj:b2RevoluteJoint;
          rj=world.CreateJoint(rJoint) as b2RevoluteJoint;
        }
        rJoint.bodyB=rearWheel;
        rJoint.localAnchorA.Set(-20/worldScale,15/worldScale);
        if (motor) {
          rrj=world.CreateJoint(rJoint) as b2RevoluteJoint;
        }
        else {
          rj=world.CreateJoint(rJoint) as b2RevoluteJoint;
        }
        return body;
    }
```

5. As we are using a custom contact listener, we'll disable collisions between the projectile and the siege machine using the `customContact` class.

6. Finally, the `updateWorld` must also be changed to include the lines to remove destroyed bodies.

```
private function updateWorld(e:Event):void {
  if (left) {
    motorSpeed-=0.1;
  }
  if (right) {
    motorSpeed+=0.1;
  }
  motorSpeed*0.99;
  if (motorSpeed>5) {
    motorSpeed=5;
  }
  if (motorSpeed<-5) {
    motorSpeed=-5;
  }
  frj.SetMotorSpeed(motorSpeed);
  rrj.SetMotorSpeed(motorSpeed);
  world.Step(1/30,10,10);
  world.ClearForces();
  for (var b:b2Body=world.GetBodyList(); b; b=b.GetNext())
  {
    if (b.GetUserData()=="remove") {
      world.DestroyBody(b);
    }
  }
  world.DrawDebugData();
}
```

7. And last but not the least, something new to learn about collisions. The following is how I am using the `PreSolve` callback function to determine if the cart collided with the projectile and disable the collision before the contact is solved, adding this function to the `customContact` class:

```
override public function PreSolve(contact:b2Contact,
oldManifold:b2Manifold):void {
  var fixtureA:b2Fixture=contact.GetFixtureA();
  var fixtureB:b2Fixture=contact.GetFixtureB();
  var dataA:String=fixtureA.GetBody().GetUserData();
  var dataB:String=fixtureB.GetBody().GetUserData();
  if (dataA=="cart" && dataB=="projectile") {
    contact.SetEnabled(false);
```

```
        }
        if (dataB=="cart" && dataA=="projectile") {
          contact.SetEnabled(false);
        }
      }
```

There's nothing you haven't already seen when you learned how to handle collisions. I just check for the cart and data to collide and disable the contact with the setEnabled method.

8. Test the movie and as promised you'll have your siege machine destroying pigs' castle.

Everything worked fine, a new game concept is ready to be expanded, and we are completely satisfied with it, aren't we?

To tell you the truth, in some cases you will notice that the projectile seems to pass through a brick without touching it. Is it a Box2D bug? Or something wrong in the contact callback? None of them, it's just a Box2D feature you haven't discovered already, but you are about to soon.

Summary

In the longest and hardest chapter of the book, you have learned how to use mouse, distance, and revolute joints to bring gameplay to higher levels. Why don't you try to build a catapult?

7
Skinning the Game

Now you are able to build playable games with Box2D, but don't expect them to be a success if you just use the built-in debug draw to render the world.

Cute graphics really make the difference between a playable game and an awesome game. Would you have more fun killing pigs with angry birds or killing gray circles with gray squares?

In this chapter you'll learn how to skin your game, in order to give it a solid personality using the following concepts:

- Replacing debug draw with your own graphic assets
- Synchronizing graphic assets with Box2D bodies' position and rotation

By the end of the chapter, you will have your Angry Birds and Totem Destroyer games skinned with your custom graphics.

Replacing debug draw with your own graphic assets

This may seem obvious, but in order to replace debug draw with your graphic assets, you will need to draw some graphic assets.

So the first question is, how many sprites do I need to draw?

Let's make a list of the actors in the Totem Destroyer game:

- Two 30 x 30 pixels breakable bricks
- One 120 x 30 pixels breakable brick
- One 90 x 30 pixels breakable brick

Skinning the Game

- One 60 x 30 pixels unbreakable brick
- One 120 x 60 pixels unbreakable brick
- The floor
- The idol

So these are the graphic assets we need to draw. Remember to draw them with the registration point at the center, to match body origin, and also remember to export them for ActionScript.

Get the latest Totem Destroyer project and start drawing. The following screenshot shows my library window. Please notice the names under **AS Linkage** as I will be using them in the code.

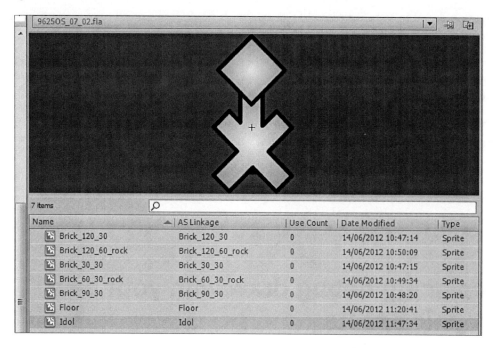

The idea is simple, we are going to use custom user data to store and handle sprites.

1. So the first step is changing how the `Main` function calls `brick`, adding a new argument, the sprite itself.

   ```
   public function Main() {
     world=new b2World(new b2Vec2(0,5),true);
     addChild(textMon);
     textMon.textColor=0xffffff;
     textMon.width=300;
     textMon.height=300;
   ```

```
textFormat.size=25;
textMon.defaultTextFormat=textFormat;
brick(275,435,30,30,"breakable",new Brick_30_30());
brick(365,435,30,30,"breakable",new Brick_30_30());
brick(320,405,120,30,"breakable",new Brick_120_30());
brick(320,375,60,30,"unbreakable",
  new Brick_60_30_rock());
brick(305,345,90,30,"breakable",new Brick_90_30());
brick(320,300,120,60,"unbreakable",
  new Brick_120_60_rock());
idol(320,242);
floor();
addEventListener(Event.ENTER_FRAME,updateWorld);
stage.addEventListener(MouseEvent.CLICK,destroyBrick);
}
```

As you can see, now every brick call includes a new instance of its sprite.

2. Changes in the `brick` function are minimal:

```
private function
brick(pX:int,pY:int,w:Number,h:Number,s:String,
asset:Sprite):void {
  var bodyDef:b2BodyDef=new b2BodyDef();
  bodyDef.position.Set(pX/worldScale,pY/worldScale);
  bodyDef.type=b2Body.b2_dynamicBody;
  bodyDef.userData=new Object();
  bodyDef.userData.name=s;
  bodyDef.userData.asset=asset;
  addChild(bodyDef.userData.asset);
  var polygonShape:b2PolygonShape=new b2PolygonShape();
  polygonShape.SetAsBox(w/2/worldScale,h/2/worldScale);
  var fixtureDef:b2FixtureDef=new b2FixtureDef();
  fixtureDef.shape=polygonShape;
  fixtureDef.density=2;
  fixtureDef.restitution=0.4;
  fixtureDef.friction=0.5;
  var theBrick:b2Body=world.CreateBody(bodyDef);
  theBrick.CreateFixture(fixtureDef);
}
```

Obviously, the function declaration now has a new argument called `asset`, but the core of the script resides in the use of the `userData` property. Rather than merely storing a string, now it's an object:

```
bodyDef.userData=new Object();
```

Skinning the Game

Now we can use the object to store anything we want, such as the name and the sprite.

```
bodyDef.userData.name=s;
bodyDef.userData.asset=asset;
```

3. Finally, we can add the sprite on the stage:

   ```
   addChild(bodyDef.userData.asset);
   ```

4. Once we apply the changes to `userData` property when creating bricks, to maintain some kind of uniformity with other bodies, we need to apply the same changes to `floor` and `idol` functions. The `floor` function is shown as follows:

   ```
   private function floor():void {
     var bodyDef:b2BodyDef=new b2BodyDef();
     bodyDef.position.Set(320/worldScale,465/worldScale);
     bodyDef.userData=new Object();
     bodyDef.userData.name="floor";
     bodyDef.userData.asset=new Floor();
     addChild(bodyDef.userData.asset);
     var polygonShape:b2PolygonShape=new b2PolygonShape();
     polygonShape.SetAsBox(320/worldScale,15/worldScale);
     var fixtureDef:b2FixtureDef=new b2FixtureDef();
     fixtureDef.shape=polygonShape;
     fixtureDef.restitution=0.4;
     fixtureDef.friction=0.5;
     var theFloor:b2Body=world.CreateBody(bodyDef);
     theFloor.CreateFixture(fixtureDef);
   }
   ```

   And the `idol` function is shown as follows:

   ```
   private function idol(pX:Number,pY:Number):void {
     var bodyDef:b2BodyDef=new b2BodyDef();
     bodyDef.position.Set(pX/worldScale,pY/worldScale);
     bodyDef.type=b2Body.b2_dynamicBody;
     bodyDef.userData=new Object();
     bodyDef.userData.name="idol";
     bodyDef.userData.asset=new Idol();
     addChild(bodyDef.userData.asset);
     var polygonShape:b2PolygonShape=new b2PolygonShape();
     polygonShape.SetAsBox(5/worldScale,20/worldScale);
     var fixtureDef:b2FixtureDef=new b2FixtureDef();
     fixtureDef.shape=polygonShape;
     fixtureDef.density=1;
   ```

```
fixtureDef.restitution=0.4;
fixtureDef.friction=0.5;
var theIdol:b2Body=world.CreateBody(bodyDef);
theIdol.CreateFixture(fixtureDef);
var bW:Number=5/worldScale;
var bH:Number=20/worldScale;
var boxPos:b2Vec2=new b2Vec2(0,10/worldScale);
var boxAngle:Number=-Math.PI/4;
polygonShape.SetAsOrientedBox(bW,bH,boxPos,boxAngle);
fixtureDef.shape=polygonShape;
theIdol.CreateFixture(fixtureDef);
boxAngle=Math.PI/4;
polygonShape.SetAsOrientedBox(bW,bH,boxPos,boxAngle);
fixtureDef.shape=polygonShape;
theIdol.CreateFixture(fixtureDef);
var vertices:Vector.<b2Vec2>=new Vector.<b2Vec2>();
vertices.push(new b2Vec2(-15/worldScale,
  -25/worldScale));
vertices.push(new b2Vec2(0,-40/worldScale));
vertices.push(new b2Vec2(15/worldScale,
  -25/worldScale));
vertices.push(new b2Vec2(0,-10/worldScale));
polygonShape.SetAsVector(vertices,4);
fixtureDef.shape=polygonShape;
theIdol.CreateFixture(fixtureDef);
}
```

5. As a new sprite is created every time a body is added to the world, we need to remove it once the body is destroyed, so we are calling a `removeChild` method in the `queryCallback` function before we destroy the body.

```
private function queryCallback(fixture:b2Fixture):Boolean {
  var touchedBody:b2Body=fixture.GetBody();
  var userData:String=touchedBody.GetUserData().name;
  if (userData=="breakable") {
    removeChild(touchedBody.GetUserData().asset);
    world.DestroyBody(touchedBody);
  }
  return false;
}
```

Now we have all sprites added and removed conveniently. The last task is to move and rotate them at every frame to follow the bodies they have been linked to.

Skinning the Game

6. This is really easy. In the `updateWorld` function, we just have to retrieve body position and rotation with `GetPosition` and `GetAngle` methods, and rotate the sprites consequently. So the new content of the `updateWorld` function is shown as follows:

```
var radToDeg:Number=180/Math.PI;
world.Step(1/30,10,10);
world.ClearForces();
if (! gameOver) {
  for (var b:b2Body=world.GetBodyList(); b;
    b=b.GetNext()) {
    if (b.GetUserData()) {
      b.GetUserData().asset.x=
        b.GetPosition().x*worldScale;
      b.GetUserData().asset.y=
        b.GetPosition().y*worldScale;
      b.GetUserData().asset.rotation=
        b.GetAngle()*radToDeg;
      if (b.GetUserData().name=="idol") {
        var position:b2Vec2=b.GetPosition();
        var xPos:Number=
          Math.round(position.x*worldScale);
        textMon.text=xPos.toString();
        textMon.appendText(",");
        var yPos:Number=
          Math.round(position.y*worldScale);
        textMon.appendText(yPos.toString());
        textMon.appendText("\nangle: ");
        var angle:Number=
          Math.round(b.GetAngle()*radToDeg);
        textMon.appendText(angle.toString());
        textMon.appendText("\nVelocity: ");
        var velocity:b2Vec2=b.GetLinearVelocity();
        var xVel:Number=
          Math.round(velocity.x*worldScale);
        textMon.appendText(xVel.toString());
        textMon.appendText(",");
        var yVel:Number=
          Math.round(velocity.y*worldScale);
        textMon.appendText(yVel.toString());
        for (var c:b2ContactEdge=b.GetContactList();
          c; c=c.next) {
          var contact:b2Contact=c.contact;
          var fixtureA:b2Fixture=contact.GetFixtureA();
          var fixtureB:b2Fixture=contact.GetFixtureB();
```

```
                    var bodyA:b2Body=fixtureA.GetBody();
                    var bodyB:b2Body=fixtureB.GetBody();
                    var userDataA:String=bodyA.GetUserData().name;
                    var userDataB:String=bodyB.GetUserData().name;
                    if (userDataA=="floor" && userDataB=="idol") {
                       levelFailed();
                    }
                    if (userDataA=="idol" && userDataB=="floor") {
                       levelFailed();
                    }
                 }
              }
           }
        }
    }
```

Again, notice I have converted radians to degrees when dealing with the `GetAngle` method.

7. Test the movie, and here is your skinned Totem Destroyer game:

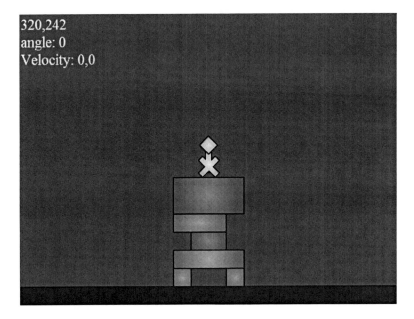

At this time, it's only a matter of designing levels.

Summary

Following this chapter, you just learned how to place your custom graphics to the Box2D world. Now you know everything you need to start making your own Box2D games. Now, follow the next chapter for some last tricks, and you'll be just one step away from developing the next big game.

8
Bullets and Sensors

You know Box2D is able to manage collisions between bodies and solve them at every step. Anyway, during the making of the siege machine in the Angry Birds prototype, something went wrong; as you probably must have noticed sometimes the projectile passes through the castle, ignoring the collision. What happened?

Normally Flash games run between 30 and 60 frames per second, and if we synchronize world step with frame rate, every step represents from 1/30 to 1/60 seconds. A simulation that relies on time steps is called **discrete simulation**, and it differs from the real world where events happen continuously, making it a **continuous simulation**.

Being a discrete simulation, we don't know what happens in the time between the nth and the $(n+1)^{th}$ step, and if a body moves really fast, it can pass through another body in less than a time step, and you'll find it on the other side of the body with no collision. This effect is called **tunneling** and we obviously want to prevent it from happening.

In this chapter you'll learn two different ways to manage contact among bodies:

- Setting bodies as bullets
- Setting bodies as sensors

By the end of the chapter, you won't have any problem managing bodies moving at high speed.

Bullets and Sensors

Experiencing tunneling

Box2D by default does its best to prevent tunneling, computing the discrete simulation using a continuous collision detection. Unfortunately, for a performance-related reason, this kind of collision detection is applied only on dynamic bodies versus static bodies. This means we can produce tunneling between two dynamic bodies.

1. Look at the following script:

    ```
    package {
      import flash.display.Sprite;
      import flash.events.MouseEvent;
      import Box2D.Dynamics.*;
      import Box2D.Collision.*;
      import Box2D.Collision.Shapes.*;
      import Box2D.Common.Math.*;
      public class Main extends Sprite {
        private var world:b2World;
        private var worldScale:Number=30;
        public function Main() {
          world=new b2World(new b2Vec2(0,5),true);
          debugDraw();
          var bodyDef:b2BodyDef=new b2BodyDef();
          bodyDef.position.Set(320/worldScale,
            470/worldScale);
          var polygonShape:b2PolygonShape=
            new b2PolygonShape();
          polygonShape.SetAsBox(320/worldScale,
            10/worldScale);
          var fixtureDef:b2FixtureDef=new b2FixtureDef();
          fixtureDef.shape=polygonShape;
          fixtureDef.density=1;
          fixtureDef.restitution=0.5;
          fixtureDef.friction=0.5;
          var body:b2Body=world.CreateBody(bodyDef);
          body.CreateFixture(fixtureDef);
          bodyDef.position.Set(600/worldScale,
            240/worldScale);
          bodyDef.type=b2Body.b2_dynamicBody;
          polygonShape.SetAsBox(10/worldScale,
            220/worldScale);
          var body2:b2Body=world.CreateBody(bodyDef);
          body2.CreateFixture(fixtureDef);
    ```

```
            bodyDef.position.Set(320/worldScale,
              455/worldScale);
            polygonShape.SetAsBox(5/worldScale,5/worldScale);
            var body3:b2Body=world.CreateBody(bodyDef);
            body3.CreateFixture(fixtureDef);
            body3.SetLinearVelocity(new b2Vec2(100,-10));
            stage.addEventListener(MouseEvent.CLICK,
              updateWorld);
        }
        private function debugDraw():void {
            var debugDraw:b2DebugDraw=new b2DebugDraw();
            var debugSprite:Sprite=new Sprite();
            addChild(debugSprite);
            debugDraw.SetSprite(debugSprite);
            debugDraw.SetDrawScale(worldScale);
            debugDraw.SetFlags(b2DebugDraw.e_shapeBit);
            debugDraw.SetFillAlpha(0.5);
            world.SetDebugDraw(debugDraw);
        }
        private function updateWorld(e:MouseEvent):void {
            world.Step(1/30,10,10);
            world.ClearForces();
            world.DrawDebugData();
        }
    }
}
```

There's nothing new in the script. It places three bodies called `body`, `body2`, and `body3`, which are respectively a static floor, a vertical dynamic barrier, and a small dynamic bullet.

As you can see, the bullet is fired at a quite high speed `(100,-10)`, and the `updateWorld` function, which runs world step, is not called at every frame but at every mouse click. This will allow you to run the simulation step by step, as slow as you want, and see what happens.

2. Test the movie and make some clicks.

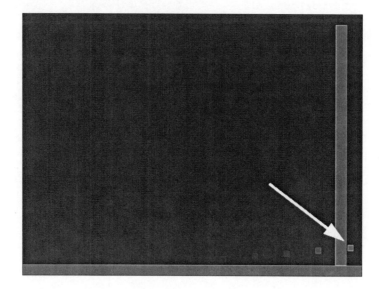

What happened? The projectile passed through the barrier without touching it. We just experienced tunneling. Now, let's make something to prevent it.

Preventing tunneling – setting bodies as bullets

As tunneling through static bodies isn't allowed thanks to continuous collision detection, in some cases we can also enable it on dynamic bodies by setting them as bullets. A bullet performs continuous collision detection with static and dynamic bodies.

Remember, you can experience heavy performance issues if you set all bodies to bullets, so it's up to you to find a compromise between accuracy and performance.

In my experience, I had to set as bullets only some particles and projectiles fired by players or enemies. Normally game characters do not move that fast to require them to be set as bullets.

1. Change the Main function by adding the highlighted line:

```
public function Main() {
    world=new b2World(new b2Vec2(0,5),true);
    debugDraw();
    var bodyDef:b2BodyDef=new b2BodyDef();
    bodyDef.position.Set(320/worldScale,470/worldScale);
    var polygonShape:b2PolygonShape=new b2PolygonShape();
    polygonShape.SetAsBox(320/worldScale,10/worldScale);
    var fixtureDef:b2FixtureDef=new b2FixtureDef();
    fixtureDef.shape=polygonShape;
    fixtureDef.density=1;
    fixtureDef.restitution=0.5;
    fixtureDef.friction=0.5;
    var body:b2Body=world.CreateBody(bodyDef);
    body.CreateFixture(fixtureDef);
    bodyDef.position.Set(600/worldScale,240/worldScale);
    bodyDef.type=b2Body.b2_dynamicBody;
    polygonShape.SetAsBox(10/worldScale,220/worldScale);
    var body2:b2Body=world.CreateBody(bodyDef);
    body2.CreateFixture(fixtureDef);
    bodyDef.position.Set(320/worldScale,455/worldScale);
    bodyDef.bullet=true;
    polygonShape.SetAsBox(5/worldScale,5/worldScale);
    var body3:b2Body=world.CreateBody(bodyDef);
    body3.CreateFixture(fixtureDef);
    body3.SetLinearVelocity(new b2Vec2(100,-10));
    stage.addEventListener(MouseEvent.CLICK,updateWorld);
}
```

Setting the bullet property in the body definition to true will enable continuous collision detection to the bullet. Now the bullet should bounce
on the barrier.

2. Test the movie and see what happens:

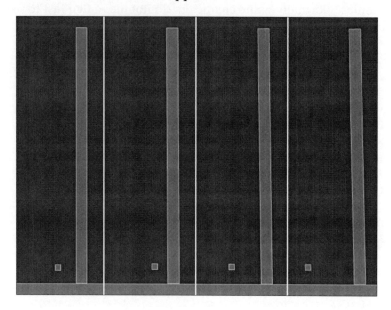

Did you see it? Now the bullet bounces on the barrier, and the contact is solved as you are used to seeing it.

3. Apply the `bullet` property to the projectile fired by the siege machine in your Angry Birds prototype, and you'll have an accurate simulation running.

Now let's see the last special type of body you can create with Box2D.

Allow bodies to overlap while detecting contacts with sensors

Sometimes in your games, you may need two bodies to overlap just like there wasn't any collision, while detecting the collision. This can be achieved using a **sensor**: a fixture that detects contacts without producing responses.

You can use sensors to create bodies so that you'll know when they collide without any physical contact between them. Just think about a character controlled by the player and a switch: you want to know when the player hits the switch to trigger some event, but at the same time you don't want the switch to react to player collision.

Chapter 8

In this last script we'll test a sensor.

1. First, add the Contacts class to the package. This is not required to create a sensor, it's just to make you see how Box2D handles sensor collision.

   ```
   import flash.display.Sprite;
   import flash.events.MouseEvent;
   import Box2D.Dynamics.*;
   import Box2D.Collision.*;
   import Box2D.Collision.Shapes.*;
   import Box2D.Common.Math.*;
   import Box2D.Dynamics.Contacts.*;
   ```

2. Then as usual, we give a name to all bodies, make the barrier static, and define its fixture as a sensor with the isSensor property.

   ```
   public function Main() {
     world=new b2World(new b2Vec2(0,5),true);
     debugDraw();
     var bodyDef:b2BodyDef=new b2BodyDef();
     bodyDef.position.Set(320/worldScale,470/worldScale);
     bodyDef.userData="floor";
     var polygonShape:b2PolygonShape=new b2PolygonShape();
     polygonShape.SetAsBox(320/worldScale,10/worldScale);
     var fixtureDef:b2FixtureDef=new b2FixtureDef();
     fixtureDef.shape=polygonShape;
     fixtureDef.density=1;
     fixtureDef.restitution=0.5;
     fixtureDef.friction=0.5;
     fixtureDef.isSensor=true;
     var body:b2Body=world.CreateBody(bodyDef);
     body.CreateFixture(fixtureDef);
     bodyDef.position.Set(600/worldScale,240/worldScale);
     bodyDef.userData="barrier";
     polygonShape.SetAsBox(10/worldScale,220/worldScale);
     var body2:b2Body=world.CreateBody(bodyDef);
     body2.CreateFixture(fixtureDef);
     bodyDef.position.Set(320/worldScale,455/worldScale);
     bodyDef.bullet=true;
     bodyDef.type=b2Body.b2_dynamicBody;
     bodyDef.userData="bullet";
     polygonShape.SetAsBox(5/worldScale,5/worldScale);
     fixtureDef.isSensor=false;
     var body3:b2Body=world.CreateBody(bodyDef);
     body3.CreateFixture(fixtureDef);
   ```

```
        body3.SetLinearVelocity(new b2Vec2(100,-10));
        stage.addEventListener(MouseEvent.CLICK,updateWorld);
}
```

Why are we making the barrier static? As it's a sensor, its collision won't be solved, so if we set it as dynamic it won't collide with the ground, falling down. Making it static will ensure us it will stay in its place.

3. Finally, we modify the `updateWorld` function in the same way you already learned when you worked on collision detection:

```
private function updateWorld(e:MouseEvent):void {
  world.Step(1/30,10,10);
  world.ClearForces();
  for (var b:b2Body=world.GetBodyList();b; b=b.GetNext()) {
    for (var c:b2ContactEdge=b.GetContactList();c; c=c.next) {
      var contact:b2Contact=c.contact;
      var fixtureA:b2Fixture=contact.GetFixtureA();
      var fixtureB:b2Fixture=contact.GetFixtureB();
      var bodyA:b2Body=fixtureA.GetBody();
      var bodyB:b2Body=fixtureB.GetBody();
      var userDataA:String=bodyA.GetUserData();
      var userDataB:String=bodyB.GetUserData();
      if (userDataA=="barrier" || userDataB=="barrier") {
        trace(userDataA+"->"+userDataB);
      }
    }
  }
  world.DrawDebugData();
}
```

4. We scan through all bodies, and for each body through all contacts, and when we find the barrier is colliding with something, we write in the output window about what happened.

5. Test the movie and make the bullet run by clicking on it:

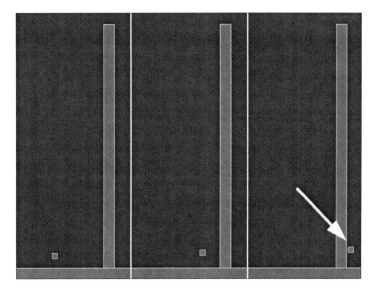

As you can see, the bullet passes through the barrier, but the collision is detected as shown from the following output text:

bullet->barrier

bullet->barrier

In this case, the message is reported twice as it's printed when scanning collisions for the projectile and finding the barrier, and when scanning collisions for the barrier and finding the projectile.

Summary

Using the two properties discussed in this chapter, you have learned how to manage continuous collision detection in a discrete simulation, and how to create passive bodies, which detect collisions without solving them.

Well, your journey into this book ends here, but there's more to learn about Box2D. You may be able to make Box2D games, but programming is a world that evolves really fast, and you should always stay up to date. I suggest you often visit `www.box2d.org` and `http://box2d.org/manual.pdf`, the official Box2D site and docs, as well as my blog `www.emanueleferonato.com` for the latest tricks and tutorials. Once you have made your first Flash Box2D game, don't forget to thank *Erin Catto* for making such an awesome library and *Boris the Brave* for porting it to AS3.

Index

A

addCart function 106
addWheel function 107
Angry Birds game
  bird, launching 67-69
  force, applying 64, 66
  physics bird, placing 70
  physics bird, shooting 71-73
Angry Birds level
  destroying, with siege machine 93
ApplyForce method 56
ApplyImpulse method 57

B

b2Body 18
b2BodyDef 16
b2CircleShape 17
b2ContactEdge 84
b2Contact object 84
b2DebugDraw 20
b2DistanceJointDef 101
b2MouseJointDef object 97
b2PolygonShape class 22
b2PolygonShape method 34
b2Vec2 object 34
Begin Contact Event 78
BeginContact function 78
birdRelease function 69
bodies. *See* Box2D body
body 15
body attributes
  assigning 27
  density 26
  friction 26
  restitution 26
bodyDef attribute 18
body properties
  getting 47-52
body types
  dynamic body 24
  kinematic body 24
  static body 24
Box2D 3, 4
Box2D body
  about 3
  body types 24
  box shape, creating 22, 23
  circular shape, creating 17
  compound bodies, creating 32, 33
  convex polygons, creating 36-40
  creating 15
  custom attributes, assigning 45-47
  fixture, creating 18, 19
  interacting with 41
  looping through, and getting
      properties 47-52
  oriented box shape, creating 34-36
  picking and dragging 93
  selecting and destroying,
      with mouse click 42-45
  setting, as bullets 140
  simulations 15
Box2D built-in collision listener 77, 78
Box2D for Flash
  downloading 4
  download links 4
  installing 4

Box2D games, skinning
  about 129
  debug draw, replacing with custom graphic assets 129-135
Box2D World
  bodies, moving using forces 53
  collisions, handling 75
  defining 5-7
boxAngle variable 34
box shape
  creating 22-24
bullet
  bodies, setting as 140-142

C

categoryBits property 121
circular shape
  creating 17
click listener 85
collision filtering 121
collisions
  checking 76, 77
  filtering 117-122
collisions management
  about 75
  Begin Contact Event, tracing 78
  Box2D built-in collision listener 77
  bricks and killing pigs, destroying in Angry Birds 85-90
  collisions, checking for 76, 77
  End Contact Event, tracing 78
  idol hitting ground, detecting 81-85
  Post-Solve Event, tracing 79
  Pre-Solve Event, tracing 79
compound bodies
  creating 32, 33
continuous simulation 137
convex polygons
  creating 36-40
createJoint callback function 95
CreateJoint method 98
custom attributes
  assigning, to bodies 45-47
customContact class 77, 124, 126

D

debug draw
  about 19
  replacing, with custom graphic assets 129-135
  used, for testing simulation 19-22
debugDraw function 99, 107
debugSprite 21
density 26
DestroyBody method 44
destroyBrick function 42
DestroyJoint method 121
discrete simulation 137
distance joints
  about 100
  creating 100-102
DrawDebugData method 19
dynamic body 24

E

enableMotor 112
End Contact Event 78
EndContact function 78
ENTER_FRAME event 8

F

falling ball, simulation
  creating 16
  gravity, configuring 16, 17
fixture
  about 18
  creating 19
floor function 38
force
  about 56
  applying, to body 56-59
  applying, to get linear velocity 61-63
  applying, to real world example 64, 66
  object, raising from ground 53, 55
frames per second (fps) 4
friction 26

G

gameOver variable 85
GetAngle method 51
GetBodyList method 50, 84
GetBody method 43
GetLinearVelocity method 51
GetPosition method 50
GetType method 95
GetWorldCenter method 56
gravity 5
ground body 97

H

Hello Box2D World 5

I

impulse
  about 57
  applying, to get linear velocity 60, 61
inelastic collision 26

J

joints
  about 93
  controlling, with motors 110-112
  distance joints 100
  mouse joints 93
  revolute joints 102

K

keyboard
  motors, controlling with 113-117
keyPressed function 121
killJoint function 98
kinematic body 24

L

levelFailed function 85
linear velocity 57

M

maxMotorTorque property 112
motors
  scontrolling, with keyboard 113-117
  joints, controlling with 110, 112
motorSpeed property 112
mouse joints
  about 94
  creating 93-98
mouseToWorld function 95, 97

O

oriented box shape
  creating 34-36

P

perfectly elastic collision 26
physics bird
  placing 70, 71
  shooting 71, 72
pig function 86
pixelsToMeters 17
position constraint solver 8
position property 16
Post-Solve Event 79
PostSolve function 80
PreSolve callback function 126
Pre-Solve Event 79
PreSolve function 80

Q

queryCallback function 43, 95, 97, 133
QueryPoint method 43

R

removeChild method 133
restitution 26
revolute joints
  about 102
  creating 102-104
rigid body 3

S

sensors
  about 142
  used, for allowing bodies overlapping detecting the collision 142-145
  used, for allowing bodies overlapping while detecting the collision 142
SetAsBox method 22
SetAsOrientedBox method 34
SetContactListener method 77
SetFillAlpha method 21
SetFlags method 21, 99
  about
SetLinearVelocity method 57, 59
SetSprite method 21
shape 17
shape attribute 22
siege machine
  about 105
  building 105-110
  implementing 122-127
  testing 122
simulation
  ball falling on floor 15
  falling ball, creating 15
  running 7-10
  testing, debug draw used 19-22

sleep 6
sphereCenter variable 56
static body 24
Step method 10, 19
switch statement 121

T

textMon 47
theBird 67
Totem Destroyer level
  creating 28-31
tunneling
  about 137
  experiencing 138
  preventing 140-142

U

updateWorld function 8, 19, 49, 107, 126, 144

V

velocity constraint solver 8

W

worldScale variable 17

Thank you for buying
Box2D for Flash Games

About Packt Publishing

Packt, pronounced 'packed', published its first book "*Mastering phpMyAdmin for Effective MySQL Management*" in April 2004 and subsequently continued to specialize in publishing highly focused books on specific technologies and solutions.

Our books and publications share the experiences of your fellow IT professionals in adapting and customizing today's systems, applications, and frameworks. Our solution based books give you the knowledge and power to customize the software and technologies you're using to get the job done. Packt books are more specific and less general than the IT books you have seen in the past. Our unique business model allows us to bring you more focused information, giving you more of what you need to know, and less of what you don't.

Packt is a modern, yet unique publishing company, which focuses on producing quality, cutting-edge books for communities of developers, administrators, and newbies alike. For more information, please visit our website: `www.packtpub.com`.

About Packt Open Source

In 2010, Packt launched two new brands, Packt Open Source and Packt Enterprise, in order to continue its focus on specialization. This book is part of the Packt Open Source brand, home to books published on software built around Open Source licenses, and offering information to anybody from advanced developers to budding web designers. The Open Source brand also runs Packt's Open Source Royalty Scheme, by which Packt gives a royalty to each Open Source project about whose software a book is sold.

Writing for Packt

We welcome all inquiries from people who are interested in authoring. Book proposals should be sent to author@packtpub.com. If your book idea is still at an early stage and you would like to discuss it first before writing a formal book proposal, contact us; one of our commissioning editors will get in touch with you.

We're not just looking for published authors; if you have strong technical skills but no writing experience, our experienced editors can help you develop a writing career, or simply get some additional reward for your expertise.

jMonkeyEngine 3.0 Beginner's Guide

ISBN: 978-1-84951-646-4   Paperback: 314 pages

Develop professional 3D games for desktop, web and mobile all in the familiar Java programming language

1. Create 3D games that run on Android devices, Windows, Mac OS, Linux desktop PCs and in web browsers – for commercial, hobbyists, or educational purposes.

2. Follow end-to-end examples that teach essential concepts and processes of game development, from the basic layout of a scene to interactive game characters.

3. Make your artwork come alive and publish your game to multiple platforms, all from one unified development environment.

Unity 3.x Scripting

ISBN: 978-1-84969-230-4   Paperback: 292 pages

Write efficient, reusable scripts to build custom characters, games environments, and control enemy AI in your Unity game

1. Make your characters interact with buttons and program triggered action sequences.

2. Create custom characters and code dynamic objects and players' interaction with them.

3. Synchronize movement of character and environmental objects.

4. Add and control animations to new and existing characters.

Please check **www.PacktPub.com** for information on our titles

Flash Game Development by Example

ISBN: 978-1-84969-090-4 Paperback: 328 pages

Build 9 classic Flash games and learn game development along the way

1. Build 9 classic games in Flash. Learn the essential skills for Flash game development.
2. Start developing games straight away. Build your first game in the first chapter.
3. Fun and fast paced. Ideal for readers with no Flash or game programming experience.
4. The most popular games in the world are built in Flash.

OGRE 3D 1.7 Application Development Cookbook

ISBN: 978-1-84951-456-9 Paperback: 306 pages

Over 50 recipes to provide world-class 3D graphics solutions with OGRE 3D

1. Dive into the advanced features of OGRE 3D such as scene querying and visibility analysis.
2. Give stunning effects to your application through suitable use of lights, special effects, and views.
3. Surf through the full spectrum of OGRE 3D animation methods and insert flashy multimedia.

Please check www.PacktPub.com for information on our titles

Lightning Source UK Ltd.
Milton Keynes UK
UKOW012308051212

203225UK00003B/109/P